Coalitions and Politics

Under the General Editorship of
Benjamin I. Page
University of Chicago

Coalitions & Politics

Barbara Hinckley
University of Wisconsin, Madison

Harcourt Brace Jovanovich, Inc.

*New York / San Diego / Chicago / San Francisco / Atlanta
London / Sydney / Toronto*

Requests for permission to make copies of any part of the work should be mailed to: Permissions, Harcourt Brace Jovanovich, Inc., 757 Third Avenue, New York, N.Y. 10017.

ISBN: 0-15-507852-6
Library of Congress Catalog Card Number: 80-84595

Printed in the United States of America

The excerpt from "Poetry" by Marianne Moore on page 147 is reprinted with permission of Macmillan Publishing Co., Inc., from *Collected Poems* by Marianne Moore, copyright 1935 by Macmillan Publishing Co., Inc., renewed 1963 by Marianne Moore and T. S. Eliot, and with permission of Faber and Faber, Ltd., Publishers, from their volume titled *The Complete Poems of Marianne Moore*.

Preface

This book is addressed to students of politics—particularly those interested in analyzing and accumulating knowledge of the subject. The study of coalitions offers an interesting and highly functional method of pursuing this analysis. In fact, politics in general may be justifiably defined as the process of coalition formation. Thus the book should be of interest to all political scientists, and to both undergraduate and graduate students.

There is, however, a problem of communication concerning coalition research. Many political scientists erroneously equate coalition theory with game theory, and therefore assume that it is primarily of interest to those trained in mathematical and formal-modeling techniques. This book will show that this is not the case—that the terms cannot be used interchangeably. Game theory includes subjects (two-person games, games of pure conflict) that are not concerned with coalition formation, while coalition research includes subjects that do not use game theory. In fact, game theory is only one of three distinct approaches available for studying coalitions. Social-psychological studies and empirical political studies also provide a rich and extensive literature on the subject. One may use—or avoid—any one approach and still do coalition research.

Coalitions and Politics illustrates the breadth of application of coalition research extending beyond the obvious cases. One can study the coalition activity that occurs in informal negotiations or bureaucratic decisions, hierarchic or egalitarian settings, single events or extended and repetitive situations. By examining this variety of situations, we can gain insights across subject boundaries, identify common actions despite superficial differences, and begin to accumulate knowledge from different areas of expertise.

This is, necessarily, an exploratory study. If the application is as broad as the study asserts, no one book can be more than a beginning. The first chapter develops the proposition that a definition of coalition activity can supply a definition of politics. The next two chapters set forth three different approaches for studying coalitions and examine some of the major problems of analysis. Chapter 4 suggests a framework for accumulating results and a system of translating coalition research into questions of political interest. Chapters 5 and 6 extend the study in time and political space. The final chapters offer specific examples of application. At each point along the way, other ideas and applications could be suggested. By proposing what could be done, the book invites other studies to extend the application.

This study was begun with the help of a Guggenheim Fellowship and support by the Graduate Research Committee of the University of Wisconsin. It developed over several years and various drafts, partial incarnations in article form, and some short regenerative periods on the shelf. Of the many people who have been helpful along the way, I wish particularly to thank Benjamin Page, William Baugh, and John Aldrich for their many valuable comments on the manuscript. My thanks also to Murray Edelman, John Kessel, Austin Ranney, Barbara Sinclair, and Eric Uslaner for their important comments on an earlier draft. Anonymous reviewers and other readers of the articles have contributed greatly in sharpening thinking and proposing extensions. Finally, I wish to thank editor Joanne Daniels, whose intelligence, talent, and humor made everything much better. None of these people, of course, are responsible for the book's shortcomings, and some of them may even disagree with portions of the emphasis and substance. Nevertheless, all have been helpful in the process of translating the idea into book form.

BARBARA HINCKLEY

Contents

II

EXTENSIONS

III

APPLICATIONS

Coalitions and Politics

I

INTRODUCTION

Chapter 1

Coalitions and Politics

When we speak of politics, we know intuitively what we mean. We recognize others who are also interested, and find common concern with a range of like events. We follow the politics of international diplomacy, congressional appropriations, or the local school board; get involved in campus politics; or applaud someone's great political skill. Yet what we recognize at the intuitive level as a commonality has not been made explicit or precise—at least not in that discipline which calls itself "Political Science." Some core insight is lacking, some conceptual base point necessary to order the information collected and identify recurrences in all the diversity and complexity of political events.

In the search for models, we have made do with metaphors—comparing politics to biological life-support systems, cybernetics, and the economic marketplace. But if *model* means a simplified schematic of the elements and processes we are interested in studying, then we have still to specify what these centrally interesting elements and processes may be. The metaphors themselves have been traced at length: there are detailed blueprints of industrial conversion processes and a brilliant account of information storage and retrieval systems and the workings of the human mind. The other side, the political side, is less clearly detailed. The area of "likeness" with the metaphor is not distinguished from the area of "unlikeness." The core insight that presumably prompted the metaphor in the first place remains elusive. The problem of recognizing political distinctiveness remains.

In this context, claims for the study of coalitions are worth more attention. These claims have been made before, but usually briefly and often tied to a particular approach attracting limited applications.[1] Some restaking may be necessary to elaborate them more fully, redefine their importance, and expand the breadth and diversity of application. This is the purpose of the present book, which proposes a remapping, both of the claims laid and the territory explored.

In short, the book proposes that a definition of coalition activity supplies a definition of politics. Coalition activity is, in fact, a "small measure" ("model," from the Latin *modulus*) of political activity, and not merely a metaphorical insight. Thus the diversity and complexity of political activity can be simplified, ordered, and subsumed by the definition, and the research devoted to coalitions can be applied to the study of politics. This briefly is the claim for the study of coalitions and the central idea of the book. To say "a definition of politics" means precisely that: not the only possible definition, not a definition of government, and not necessarily a definition of what political scientists may be currently studying. The overlap with these areas is substantial, but not complete. In some ways, the definition broadens attention beyond traditional spheres; in other ways, it concentrates it more narrowly. It involves a shift in perspective—a different point of view—that should bring into clearer focus the question of distinctiveness and what these "centrally interesting elements and processes" may be.

A DEFINITION

A coalition has been defined as "the joint use of resources to determine the outcome of a mixed-motive situation involving more than two units."[2] A mixed-motive situation is further defined as one in which "there is an element of conflict, since there exists no outcome which maximizes the payoff to everybody. There is an element of coordination, since there exists for at least two of the players [or actors] the possibility that they can do better by coordinating their resources than by acting alone." The definition, first proposed by William Gamson and widely accepted in coalition research, deserves a fresh look and a broader point of view.

The definition calls attention to three components: (1) *an application of power* (in the sense of applying resources to determine outcomes),[3] (2) *a*

---

[1] See William Riker, *The Theory of Political Coalitions* (New Haven: Yale University Press, 1962), pp. 9–11.

[2] William Gamson, "Experimental Studies of Coalition Formation," in *Advances in Experimental Social Psychology*, ed. Leonard Berkowitz (New York: Academic Press, 1964), 1:85.

[3] The word *power* can be defined as (1) the "possession of control, authority, or influence over others" or (2) the "ability to act to produce an effect." While the first definition is frequently used in political science (for summary and comment, see David Easton, *The Political Sys-*

combination of conflict and coordination (in the mixed-motive situation), and (3) *a collective activity* (one involving joining the resources of more than two units). People confront, with others, a particular kind of situation in which an outcome must be "determined." As rational individuals, they seek to maximize their own returns. But to do this, they must work with others who are also trying to maximize their own returns; and the situation provides no outcome that maximizes the returns to everyone. We can assume, with other writers, that these people are conscious of being in the situation.[4] Coalition actors consciously join resources, work in a mixed-motive situation, and apply power to determine outcomes; and they assume that the other actors are similarly aware. The awareness may be tacit or explicit. Information may be excellent or poor. One need not think well or correctly about the situation, but one is aware of being in it—of being engaged in coalition activity. If one person uses the action (or vote or position) of another to gain more than he or she would otherwise, and does it without that person's knowledge, they have not formed a coalition. To form a coalition, both partners must be aware that they could gain more by working together than by working alone.

Now match these three components against any common sense usage of the word *politics*. A palace coup, a constitutional convention, a legislative vote, a budget decision, a presidential nomination—actions as unlike one another as these are subsumed by the definition. It does not restrict activity by size of stakes, kind of setting, or form of organization. Resources can be employed in groups of three or three hundred, by individuals or nations, in structures that are egalitarian or hierarchical, personalistic or institutionalized. Coalitions occur with Latin American elites, American civil rights groups, the European Economic Community, precolonial African nations, legislative log rolls, and multiparty cabinet formation.[5] Nor does the definition restrict activity to a particular point in time. Coalition actors may be engaged in bargaining about possible coalitions, forming temporary coalitions and disbanding them, or maintaining a present satisfactory alliance. Certainly, the definition embraces a breadth and diversity of political action and political forms.

Going somewhat further, it might be suggested that the *collective mixed-motive situation is precisely the kind of human problem that calls for political skills*. Pure conflict tends toward war, fistfights, or total noninteraction; pure coordination toward friendship, teamwork, or wholly supportive alliances. The pure cases call for other human activity. In the area between

---

tem, 2nd ed. [New York: Alfred Knopf, 1971], pp. 143, 144), it is the second, more general definition that is implied in the phrase "to determine the outcome of a situation." Coalition actors join resources to produce an effect—to determine an outcome—in a particular kind of situation.

[4] See Gamson, *Experimental Studies of Coalition Formation*, and Riker, *Political Coalitions*.

[5] See, for example, the studies in Sven Groennings et al., eds., *The Study of Coalition Behavior* (New York: Holt, Rinehart and Winston, 1970).

the war and the full alliance, the friendship and the fistfights, the exercise of power that we call "political" comes into play.[6] Bargaining, compromise, mobilization of support, majority rule, activity from summit to grass roots—all of these start from and attempt to deal with mixed-motive affairs.

In other words, a common understanding of political activity includes (1) individuals or groups engaged in *collective* activity, in interaction with more than one other; (2) the *exercise of power*—the use, organization, and application of resources to gain certain ends; and (3) that area of human affairs in which *no solutions of pure conflict or pure coordination obtain*. The three components are necessary and sufficient to the coalition definition. They may be similarly necessary and sufficient to a political definition, as shown by the simple exercise of trying to imagine a purely "political" activity without one of the three, or seeing how events become political by adding the third component to any other two.

For example, situations involving power and conflict and coordination without collective action (components 2 and 3 without 1) include individual calculations or psychological conflicts, but are not necessarily political. Collective situations involving both conflict and coordination without concern for the exercise of power (components 1 and 3 without 2) are social but not necessarily political—many games, competitions, some cocktail party conversations. Collective exercises of power involving only conflict or only coordination (components 1 and 2 without 3) are also social but not necessarily political—a free-for-all, an orchestrated public relations campaign, coordination of the football team, conflict between the teams. Combining the three, however, produces a "political" situation: combining individuals with cross-purposes into a collective decision-making process; adding to the cocktail party conversation the element of some exercise of power; adding conflict or coordination to a situation where only the other is present, thus producing the "politics" of the football locker room or the public relations campaign. Indeed, the three components should help to distinguish political activity from other psychological and social human affairs.

Human beings engage in rational calculations to maximize their own returns. They also engage in social interaction—communicating and compromising with others. In neither case are they necessarily engaging in politics. They do engage in political activity when they must use rational calculation and social interaction to determine the outcome of a situation in which no solutions of pure conflict or pure coordination are possible.

The definition, however, does not entirely accord with what political

---

[6] Cf. Austin Ranney, *The Governing of Men*, 3rd ed. (New York: Holt, Rinehart and Winston, 1971), pp. 20, 21: "a political system encompasses not only competing demands and interests but also aggregative and integrative forces as well." Ranney quotes Rousseau, *Social Contract*, bk. 2, chap. 1: "What made the establishment of society necessary was, if you like, the fact that the interests of individuals clashed. But what made their establishment possible was the fact that these same interests *also* coincided."

scientists study. It excludes some traditional subject matter and it includes others typically considered outside the political sphere. In short, it shifts attention to those recurring patterns that span fields traditionally described.

The Definition and Traditional Political Science

Political scientists often study processes that are not concerned with applying power for outcomes (nondecisional processes), that are not concerned with collective activity (individual attitudes, strategic calculations, acts by absolute despots), and that do not combine elements of conflict and coordination (purely consensual processes, total wars with only two sides). In short, they study some acts of government, such as those of absolute despots, that do not involve coalition formation. Recognize that the terms *government* and *politics* are not synonymous either. Absolute despots, by definition, can determine outcomes *without* acting within a collective mixed-motive situation—in other words, *without* engaging in a process of coalition formation, or in yet other words *without having to "play politics."*

The point may be clarified by comparing the present definition with a currently popular one. David Easton has suggested "that political research is distinctive because it has been trying to reveal the way in which values are affected by authoritative allocation."[7] Since all social scientists, Easton admitted, may be interested in the allocation of values, he stressed the word "authoritative" as the distinctively political qualifier. "Authoritative" was further defined to mean "society-wide" and an authority that "people feel they must or ought to obey."[8] Yet by this definition "authoritative" comes very close to a synonym for "governmental."[9] If we substitute the one word for the other, we find political scientists distinctively concerned with governmental allocation of values—which circles us back to ask what government is or distinctively does.

In contrast, the present definition suggests that the distinctively *political* (not governmental) qualifiers for allocating values or determining outcomes are the joining of resources in collective mixed-motive situations. Of course, if one wishes to narrow the term merely to governmental application, one may, like Easton, add the word "authoritative" too.

William Riker offered a slightly different definition of coalition activ-

---

[7] Easton, *Political System*, p. 132.

[8] *Ibid.*

[9] Notice that Easton distinguishes his concept of "authoritative" from the concept of "state" and not of "government," arguing that values may be allocated by informal as well as formal (i.e., "state") institutions. If one agrees with Easton that governing occurs through both formal and informal operation, then the concept of "government," like the concept "authoritative," would be differentiated from the concept of "state."

ity, which also overlaps with "what political scientists study." According to Riker, the central activity of politics is decision-making; decisions are made either by individuals or by the quasi-mechanical or conscious processes of groups; and decisions made by the conscious actions of groups are made through the process of coalition formation.[10] Riker's formulation is like the present definition in stipulating collective action and assuming consciousness, and unlike it in shifting the exercise of power to decision-making[11] and omitting the requirement of a mixed-motive situation. Both formulations are similar in isolating a distinctive activity for study, whether the activity be by "authoritative" (i.e., governmental) actors or not. By contrast, definitions of government emphasize the authority of the actors, whatever their activity. The overlap is substantial, but not complete.

In this tracing of overlap, however, it is important not to exclude too much. What at first glance appear to be individual or two-person decisions can be analyzed as part of larger, n-person coalition situations. Individual presidents make decisions as part of a situation involving the conflict and coordination of advisers, competing support groups, and separate clienteles. They are exercising power in collective, mixed-motive situations. Nations X and Y decide to go to war or to sign a mutually advantageous trade agreement. But if the decision involves other nations Z, . . . n, this becomes a problem of coalition formation. For example, nation X supports and nation Y opposes nation Z, even though X and Y may feel neutral to each other. If Y and Z go to war, they may each bargain for X's support and X and Y may go to war in the XZ coalition against Y.

Political scientists J. David Singer and Melvin Small study the relationship of war and alliance between nation-pairs, assuming that "every dyadic [i.e., two-nation] relationship will be a mixture of the cooperative and the conflictful." Thus

> A and B may well have competing economic interests in the Middle East, but harmonious strategic interests in the Caribbean, while B and C's political interests may coincide in regard to West Africa and clash in an international organization setting.[12]

[10] Riker, *Political Coalitions*, p. 11.

[11] Riker finds "power" too vague and seeks to avoid using it (see *Political Coalitions*, p. 22). He uses instead the word "decision-making." Decision-making itself is defined by reference to Easton as "authoritative decisions on the allocation of values" (p. 11)—in other words, as governmental decisions. In many cases, Riker's decision-making will be the same as our "determining outcomes." However, our definition is not limited to governmental decisions; also, some decisions do not translate into outcomes. So, President John Kennedy decided to remove the U.S. missiles from Turkey (three times), but the missiles stayed. Kennedy had not joined resources with others to determine his desired outcome. In terms of our definition, he had not succeeded in forming a coalition.

[12] J. David Singer and Melvin Small, "Alliance Aggregation and the Onset of War, 1815–1945," in *Alliances*, ed. Francis A. Beer (New York: Holt, Rinehart and Winston, 1970), p. 16.

Singer and Small's "mixture of the cooperative and the conflictful" is another way of describing a mixed-motive situation. With this assumption comes the possibility of extending the dyad to a more-than-two-person coalition situation. Indeed, any two-nation choice between alliance and war depends in part on the cooperation and conflict with other nations. Nation B, for example, faces a critical choice of coalition partner if A and C ever clash in the Caribbean—or find a common purpose in the Middle East.

Even indifferent parties can transform the dyad into a coalition situation. All that is required, Theodore Caplow argued, is a "witness" or "potential intervenor" powerful enough to tip the balance between the two.[13] Neutrals, bystanders, or any observers are thus potential actors in a coalition situation. Two nations initiate or limit hostilities with an eye toward potential conflict and coordination with other nations. By this argument, many two-person situations need to be analyzed as part of a wider process of coalition formation.

Even the more obviously excluded areas of traditional political science have important implications for political coalitions. Individual attitude studies help explain the initial distribution of resources that is brought to a collective situation: for example, citizen support for candidates in a political campaign. Consensual processes explain how rules of the game are set for different types of coalition situations. Nondecisional processes may be outcomes of prior coalition activity where the "decision" was not to repeat the opportunity for a decision. Indeed, study of these areas may be critical *primarily because they define the rules and resources for, and regulate the occurrence of, political coalition situations.* They become critical factors affecting coalition activity and results.

At the extremes are the cases of pure conflict and pure coordination that do not pose coalition situations, and yet even these should not be too quickly disregarded. The change into or out of a coalition situation describes how a political situation (or system or particular government) begins and ends.

How, for example, is the conflict or coordination first introduced or finally eliminated? How important is membership change—adding or subtracting people who are like or unlike others? What are the conditions that terminate coalition situations, make a group of nations close communication, abandon bargaining, and turn to total war?

In short, there would seem to be a more and a less conservative delineation of the overlap possible. Some could say more conservatively that coalition activity involves a substantial part, but only a part, of political activity. Some could say less conservatively that applications of power in collective mixed-motive situations can define the activity and point to its distinctive characteristics.

---

[13] Theodore Caplow, *Two Against One: Coalitions in Triads* (Englewood Cliffs, N.J.: Prentice-Hall, 1968), pp. 148–49.

Coalitions also occur in contexts that are not traditionally considered political. In a brilliant essay, sociologist Theodore Caplow argued that social interaction is primarily triangular rather than linear and can be analyzed as the coalition activity of "two against one."[14] He identified a number of common triadic relations including the following:

leader-lieutenant-follower	two insiders-one outsider
master-journeyman-apprentice	parents and child
manager-foreman-worker	married couple and in-law

The factory foreman confronts a problem of coalition formation, since he shares elements of conflict and coordination with management on the one hand and the workers on the other, and faces a set of incentives and threats from both. A similar problem exists in the family, with age and sex the major sources of conflict and coordination, and the changing power of family members the main determinant of which coalitions form. Caplow traced a hypothetical family history from a mother-child coalition against the father, to a democratic situation where all coalitions are equally likely, to the time when mother and father realize, with a growing adolescent child, that there are advantages to a parental coalition. In some cases, rules are developed in order to inhibit the formation of some coalitions—for example, the military restriction on fraternizing between officers and enlisted men. In other cases, the rules are informal though no less powerful—as in the case of seniority norms or taboos about mothers-in-law. In all cases, the rules of the game and the particular coalitions formed will determine outcomes both for the individual lives and the social unit as a whole.

Coalitions, then, can form in the factory, the family, the army—in any kind of social interaction including but not restricted to politics. Some may say that this is really "army politics" or "factory politics"—or precisely what we mean by such popular usage of the term. Again, the extent of overlap may be more or less conservatively defined.

APPLICATION

Whether one accepts the more or the less conservative interpretations, coalition activity provides a model of political activity of considerable simplicity and breadth of application. It consists of mixed-motive actors (indi-

[14] Ibid.

viduals or groups) who work with initial resources and the rules of a game and attempt to determine an outcome and distribute returns.

These components, it is clear, comprise much of the traditional subject matter of political science and can be easily paralleled by a number of political descriptions. Initial resources may include any political resources: as Robert Dahl described them, "means by which one person can influence the behavior of other persons . . . money, information, food, the threat of force, jobs, friendship, social standing, the right to make laws, votes, and a great variety of other things."[15] They include oil, missile stockpiles, delegate votes, the number of partisans in a legislature. The rules may be formal or informal—as in constitutional law or legislative norms. A game may occur with the rules and initial resources decided, or a prior game may have determined what the subsequent resource distribution and rules of the game would be. "The study of government," said one political writer, "is the study of a particular set of rules in a most intriguing sort of game. And generally the stakes are high."[16] Another observed: "The rules of the game determine the requirements for success. Resources sufficient for success in one game may be wholly inadequate in another. These considerations go to the heart of political strategy."[17] Actors may work from private or public sectors, as in the politics of multinational corporations, and form coalitions that span, blur, or redefine both sectors. California orange growers, domestic sugar refiners, and Boeing aircraft personnel, as many case studies make clear, are very much "in politics." Thus a coalition between regulators and those regulated may be both the outcome of such a political (i.e., coalition) process and a redefinition of resources for subsequent political situations. We can then examine by what processes and under what conditions actors combine resources (or choose not to combine them) to allocate values or to determine "who gets what"[18]—*what* including such values as status, ideological satisfaction, symbolic rewards, as well as material gains. *What* may also include pollution control, peace, potato subsidies, *coups d'état*, or cabinet posts.

It should be clear that such activity need be neither discontinous nor sporadic. It is by no means limited to isolated flurries of coalition formation. The process of determining rules and resources can be extended over time. Bargaining can take years. The returns distributed from one situation may constrain and redefine the resources and rules for another. Hence at any one point in time, political actors would tend to be engaged in some

[15] Robert Dahl, *Modern Political Analysis*, rev. ed. (Englewood Cliffs, N.J.: Prentice-Hall, 1971), p. 37.
[16] Lewis Froman, Jr., "Politics in Everyday Life," in *Readings in Modern Political Analysis*, ed. Robert Dahl and Deane Neubauer (Englewood Cliffs, N.J.: Prentice-Hall, 1968), p. 33.
[17] E. E. Shattschneider, *The Semi-Sovereign People* (New York: Holt, Rinehart and Winston, 1960), pp. 48–49.
[18] Harold Lasswell, *Politics: Who Gets What, When, and How* (New York: McGraw-Hill, 1936).

stage of this activity and, commonly, at several stages in several interconnected coalition situations.

Consider the parallels between these coalition components and the following traditional political description from an essay entitled "Politics in Everyday Life":

> The important point, however, is that all are political decisions, that is, all involve the distribution of advantages and disadvantages among people with different resources. Our task is to see how people convert resources into influence, how the play of influence and counter-influence determines outcomes, and how outcomes distribute payoffs to various citizens and groups. This is the study of politics.[19]

More explicit parallels have been drawn by other writers investigating particular political subjects. They range from more to less obvious cases of application, from coalitions in multiparty cabinet formation to Southern secession.

Cabinet Formation in Multiparty Systems

> If different governments, varying in party membership and policy, may result from a given election outcome, either there is no "verdict of the electorate" or . . . the verdict is not necessarily, or even usually realized in multi-party systems. The coalition theory that could shed light on these questions would have great importance for democratic theory.[20]

Nuclear Test Ban Treaty

> U.S.-Sino-Soviet affairs [may be seen] as a multiphase three-person game in which rewards accrue to the pair that forms on each play of the game. A play, in the abstract game, consists of the three players making choices and forming a pair; a play of the game in international relations consists of the players—nations—uniting to effect some decision, for example, the signing of a test ban treaty.[21]

Presidential Nominations

> [Given] the complexity and indeterminancy of the nomination process. . . . No single group is large enough to act decisively without considerable help from other groups. In the party out of power there are no party leaders who can dominate the process or compel it to take a given course. . . . Yet the same features that inhibit intuitive understanding of nomination politics facilitate its analysis in terms of coalition formation.[22]

[19] Froman, "Politics in Everyday Life," p. 42.
[20] Abram DeSwaan, *Coalition Theories and Cabinet Formation* (San Francisco: Jossey-Bass, 1973), pp. 1, 2.
[21] Bernhardt Lieberman, "The Sino-Soviet Pair: Coalition Behavior from 1921 to 1965," in *Sino-Soviet Relations and Arms Control*, ed. Mortin Halperin (Cambridge, Mass.: M.I.T. Press, 1967), p. 326.
[22] James Zais and John Kessel, "A Theory of Presidential Nominations with a 1968 Illustration," in *Perspectives on Presidential Selection*, ed. Donald Matthews (Washington, D.C.: Brookings, 1973), p. 121.

Precolonial Africa

Coalition formation for the purpose of making temporarily binding societal decisions is not just a recent or Western phenomenon. It occurred as long ago as precolonial times and in such settings as Ganda politics.[23]

Coalitions in a Two-Party Legislature

In the absence of an overwhelming consensus on either the need for or the precise form of federal action, conflicts over policy are represented in the congressional parties, splitting them into blocs and factions that have to be accommodated before Congress can make any decision at all. Majorities are built in Congress, not elected to it; hence congressional politics is coalition politics.[24]

Southern Secession

The South's problem was the more fundamental one of an actor being transformed from an equal in a coalition situation to a permanent minority in a two-person game. . . . it is anticipation of inadequate future strength that causes minority coalitions to drop out of the game while they have sufficient capacity to effect a withdrawal.[25]

Harold Lasswell has called political science "the study of the shaping and sharing of power."[26] Joining resources to determine outcomes could also be described as a shaping and sharing of power. But we may be particularly concerned with this power shaping and power sharing in a collective context and one involving both conflict and coordination. Whatever one's definition of choice for political subject matter (including the choice of no one particular choice), one can recognize a considerable convergence in concern.

This is the conservative interpretation. There is a substantial, though not complete, convergence between the study of politics and the study of coalitions. Thus the model should be useful in organizing and analyzing political phenomena.

Less conservatively, one could say the following. The definition directs attention, once we think about it, to what we study anyway. We are interested in that kind of human activity that is collective—that occurs within and as a part of society. But more particularly, we are concerned with the exercise of power in that activity—the joining and application of resources to determine outcomes. And still more particularly, we are concerned with the exercise of power in situations combining conflict and coordination, combining the clashing and coinciding of interests—where people clash too

[23] Martin Southwold, "Riker's Theory and the Analysis of Coalitions in Precolonial Africa," in *Study of Coalition Behavior*, p. 336.

[24] John Manley, "The Conservative Coalition in Congress," *American Behavioral Scientist* 7 (Nov./Dec. 1973), p. 224.

[25] Dean Yarwood, "A Failure in Coalition Maintenance: The Defection of the South Prior to the Civil War," in *Study of Coalition Behavior*, p. 234.

[26] Harold Lasswell and Abraham Kaplan, *Power and Society* (New Haven: Yale University Press, 1950), p. xiv.

much to form a team and coincide too much to go to war. It's that common and critical problem occurring when people share a planet together. These three in combination should help distinguish political activity from other human affairs.

SUMMARY

The claim, then, for applying coalitions to politics rests on the persuasiveness of the definition. To define is to make both *determinate* and *distinctive*—to supply the boundaries of something as well as to specify its distinctive character or constituents.[27] If coalition activity, as here defined, can be viewed as a "small measure" of political activity, then it should be precisely as broad and distinctive in application as the area to which it is applied. No critique of other models is appropriate here, but it is clear that none offers the same determinateness and distinctiveness. Some give great conceptual clarity to a particular political subject, but they are not comprehensive and make no claim to be so. Others are overly comprehensive. A multitude of life forms beyond the political varieties exhibit structure and function, efficient exchanges of matter and energy, system, and a set of self-maintaining and self-regulating mechanisms. Politics may be "like" the solar system or the monetary system or the circulation of blood in the body in many heuristic, analytically stimulating ways, but nothing politically distinctive or determinate is indicated.

The limits on the claim should also be recognized. It is offered as a point of view—and a useful one—in a field that accommodates, even encourages, often insists on, many points of view. So as merely one among many, it can be compared for its usefulness, judged for its breadth and precision, and engaged for its insights with others.

---

[27] To "define," according to *Webster's Third New International Dictionary*, is "to mark the limits of: determine with precision or exhibit clearly the boundaries of . . . determine the essential qualities of." According to the *Oxford English Dictionary*, it is "to state precisely or determinately; to specify; to state exactly what (a thing) is; to set forth or explain the essential nature of. . . ."

Chapter 2

Major Approaches to Studying Coalitions

We have claimed that coalitions are central to political and social phenomena. One scholar (Riker) assigned a major portion of all political activity to coalitions. Another (Caplow) asserted even more broadly that social interaction could be viewed as the coalition activity of "two against one." The preceding chapter was no less assertive, and even a more skeptical critic would probably admit that the application of power in collective mixed-motive situations is an important and frequent part of political affairs.

It is curious, then, that the broad claims of applicability have been met by such limited political application. William Riker's work, advanced in 1962, traced the broad importance of the coalition model in the first few pages and then devoted the rest of the book to *one very specific proposition which could be derived from it.*[1] That proposition was the size principle— which will be examined in more detail later in this chapter. Seen from one point of view, this principle is merely a brilliant illustration of the larger claim. Yet most of the political science research on the subject since that date has focused only on that specific proposition, "testing" and elaborating the size principle in various political settings.

There are, in fact, three distinct approaches used in research on coalitions: (1) the social-psychological studies, (2) the game-theoretic studies, and (3) the empirical political studies. Yet the authors of the empirical political studies appear almost totally unfamiliar with the social-psychological work and refer to game theory primarily for the size principle. Fully one-half of their studies address this one research subject (see Bibliography).

---

[1] William Riker, *The Theory of Political Coalitions* (New Haven: Yale University Press, 1962).

If we are to use coalitions for the study of politics, we need to see the full range of approaches available. This chapter, then, outlines each of these approaches and examines their major techniques of analysis.

SOCIAL-PSYCHOLOGICAL STUDIES

One contribution to the study of coalitions has come from the fields of sociology and social psychology—particularly from the work of George Simmel, Theodore Caplow, and William Gamson. This approach is both *theoretical* and *empirical*: it is theoretical in that it seeks to identify and explain recurring patterns of coalition behavior, but it is empirical in that it concentrates on how coalition players actually do behave in the real world under different conditions. The theory develops with and depends for its support on evidence from concrete events. William Gamson called this work *descriptive theory*:

> A theory of coalition formation should tell us who will join with whom and how they will divide the rewards. Only those theories which are descriptive, or can be interpreted as such, will be considered here; prescriptions to the participants on how they should behave will be treated only through the addition of assumptions which translate them into predictions of how participants actually will behave.[2]

It does not matter whether we use the term descriptive theory or empirical theory: the point is that the theory draws its support from, and must be returned to, empirical results.

The main technique has been *experimental*. The researcher designs and manipulates the setting to observe results rather than observing a naturally occurring situation. For example, a researcher constructs a problem in a situation similar to a political convention, rather than attending an actual convention. The possibilities and limits of the experimental technique will be discussed further in a later chapter.

Studies of Coalition Behavior

A major impetus for this research was a theoretical paper by Theodore Caplow proposing that the formation of coalitions "depends upon the initial dis-

---

[2] William Gamson, "Experimental Studies of Coalition Formation," in *Advances in Experimental Social Psychology*, ed. Leonard Berkowitz (New York: Academic Press, 1964), 1:86.

Figure 2.1   Six Types of Triads

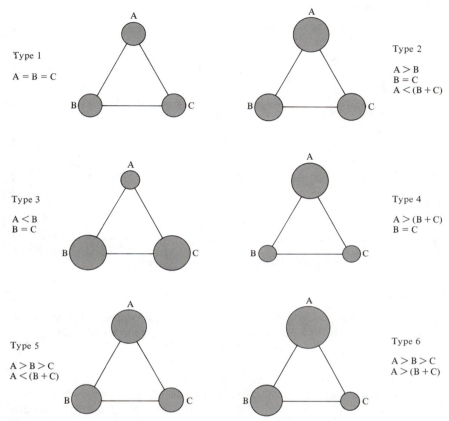

Type 1

A = B = C

Type 2

A > B
B = C
A < (B + C)

Type 3

A < B
B = C

Type 4

A > (B + C)
B = C

Type 5

A > B > C
A < (B + C)

Type 6

A > B > C
A > (B + C)

Source: Theodore Caplow, "Further Development of a Theory of Coalitions in the Triad," *American Journal of Sociology* 64 (March 1959): 488-93. Reprinted by permission of the University of Chicago Press. © 1959 by the University of Chicago.

tribution of power, and, other things being equal, may be predicted under certain assumptions when the initial distribution of power is known."[3] Caplow worked with triads: groups of three players, who may be individuals or collectivities, which he designated A, B, and C. These could be three parties in a legislature, three nations in an international system, or any other set of actors faced with the problem of joining resources in a mixed-motive situation. He identified various triadic types (see Figure 2.1) distinguished by

[3] Theodore Caplow, "A Theory of Coalitions in the Triad," *American Sociological Review* 21 (August 1956):489–92, and "Further Development of a Theory of Coalitions in the Triad," *American Journal of Sociology* 64 (March 1959):488–93.

Table 2.1 Results of Vinacke-Arkoff Experiment: Frequency of Coalition Formation for Six Triadic Types

	TRIADIC TYPES					
	1 A=B=C	2 A>B B=C A<(B+C)	3 A<B B=C	4 A>(B+C) B=C	5 A>B>C A<(B+C)	6 A>B>C A>(B+C)
COALITION	NUMBER OF TIMES A COALITION FORMED					
AB	33	13	24	11	9	9
AC	17	12	40	10	20	13
BC	30	64	15	7	59	8
No Coalition	10	1	11	62	2	60
Total	90	90	90	90	90	90

Source: W. E. Vinacke and A. Arkoff, "An Experimental Study of Coalitions in the Triad," *American Sociological Review* 22 (1957): 409. Reprinted by permission.

the initial distribution of resources among the players, and predicted what coalitions would form under these different initial resource conditions.

W. E. Vinacke and A. Arkoff tested Caplow's predictions for six of his eight triadic types.[4] The results are intriguing both for the consistencies they show and the questions that remain. The outcomes for types 4 and 6 are quite understandable: when all three players realize that a coalition cannot win against A, coalitions tend not to form. In types 2 and 5, minimum winning coalitions tend to form, although there are some exceptions. (B+C is the minimum-winning coalition, possessing fewer resources than A+C or A+B, but enough to win against A alone.) The type 1 and type 3 results, however, are less easily understood. We can wonder, for instance, why the AC coalition formed so frequently in type 3 and so infrequently in type 1.

Much of the more recent work done has been devoted to explaining and clarifying these early results.[5] It has not been limited, however, to triads (although these are still the most frequent situations examined), nor to Caplow's own initial predictions. The initial distribution of resources remains the major predictor, but the theories and experiments have sought to identify other factors overriding this influence in importance.

[4] W. E. Vinacke and A. Arkoff, "An Experimental Study of Coalitions in the Triad," *American Sociological Review* 22 (1957):406–14.
[5] For review of this research and the discussion in this section, see Barry Collins and Bertram Raven, "Group Structure: Attraction, Coalitions, Communication, and Power," in *The Handbook of Social Psychology,* 2nd ed., ed. Gardner Lindzey and Elliot Aronson, (Reading, Mass.: Addison-Wesley, 1969); vol. 4, esp. pp. 127–37.

This recent work is frequently reviewed under four headings, suggested by Gamson, each characterized by some theoretical argument and experimental results.[6] Gamson labeled them (1) minimum-resource theory, (2) minimum-power theory, (3) anticompetitive theory, and (4) "utter confusion" theory, or random choice.

Minimum-resource theory emphasizes the initial resources the players bring to the situation. It assumes that players seek to maximize their share of success from the situation and that they expect the operation of a parity norm (parity means a share of the payoff commensurate with the resources players bring to the coalition). It predicts that a coalition will form in which the total resources are as small as possible yet still sufficient to win. In a typical experiment with a political convention game in which candidate A controls 40 votes, candidate B controls 30 votes, and candidate C has 20 votes, the minimum winning coalition BC is predicted. Strength turns into weakness as initially strongest player A is excluded from the winning coalition. Minimum-resource theory receives some experimental support although in a number of cases there are discrepancies from the predicted results.

Minimum-power theory, an adaptation of game theory, emphasizes the relative power of the players rather than their initial distribution of resources. Players' "pivotal" power is the proportion of times their resources can change a losing coalition into a winning one. Rather than expecting parity, players will expect a share of the payoff proportional to their pivotal power. Thus in the political convention example, when each player has equal opportunity to change a losing coalition into a winning one, the relative power of the candidates is equal even though their initial resources differ. In such a game, minimum-power theory predicts that all coalitions are equally likely. Experimental tests of the theory have not shown strong support.

Anticompetitive theory appears to have developed mainly from the experimental discrepancies found for the minimum-resource predictions. Attitudes about competition and bargaining, personality differences, and other factors may lead players to form coalitions larger than minimum size. It predicts that "coalitions will form along the lines of least resistance: i.e., between those partners for whom there exists the most obvious and unambiguous solution to the problem of dividing the relative share of the payoff."[7] Gamson suggested that players equal in resources would form coalitions; he did not suggest what would happen with an unequal resource distribution. Clearly, this is less a theory than a single postulate, not completely specified, about coalition behavior. It is one, however, that can account for a number of experimental results.

---

[6] See ibid.; and Gamson, "Experimental Studies of Coalition Formation."
[7] Gamson, "Experimental Studies of Coalition Formation," pp. 90–91.

Utter confusion theory, or random choice, is the final research category. According to Gamson, there are some experimental results for which this is the most convincing explanation:

> Many coalition situations are conducted under conditions which are not conducive to rational calculation and analysis. . . . Thus according to this theory, coalition formation is best understood as an essentially random choice process. The coalition that forms will be the result of such fortuitous events as a chance encounter or telephone call.[8]

Unfortunately, under a number of conditions, random choice makes the same predictions as the other formulations. In the political convention game, for instance, it predicts with minimum-power theory that all coalitions are equally likely.

CRITIQUE AND ANALYSIS Despite the reference to theory, it is clear that there are no systematic or logical distinctions made between the categories. At times they overlap and at times diverge in their assumptions about the player's goals, the distribution of payoffs, and the conditions for bargaining. At some points they predict the same results. Some, as in the case of anticompetitive theory, appear to have been hastily constructed to shelter a set of otherwise anomalous results. They appear most useful in summarizing and categorizing a large amount of empirical research findings. They are an attempt to bring together a developing empirical effort and to put forth the first probes of a theory on the subject.

One line of inquiry can be suggested from this research that may be worth pursuing further. Note that each of the four "theories" identify what could be called a *salient cue for decision* in a coalition situation, where the cue is some kind of information about the players. Some kinds of information are highlighted more than others. In the minimum-resource case, it is the players' perception of their initial resource differences. In the minimum-power case, it is their perception that despite initial resource differences, they have an equal chance (or some different chance) in forming coalitions. Initial resources are still used to calculate a player's chance to form winning coalitions, but another perception has been added. The anticompetitive case simply states that the most salient cue—other than one based on initial resources—will be decisive. The random choice case states essentially that there are no salient cues—or too many to choose from.

This means, then, that players may (1) perceive the implications of initial resource differences (minimum-resource theory); (2) reject these implications in favor of some other more important kinds of information (minimum-power or anticompetitive theories); or (3) not perceive these implications or any alternative implications (random choice). Using this logical and systematic distinction between the categories, researchers can look for

[8] Ibid., p. 92.

the kinds of situational factors that highlight these perceptions. This idea will be pursued in more detail in later chapters.

Example: Social-Psychological Studies and a Political Convention

Jerome Chertkoff has argued that the probability of future success may prompt a weaker player to join with a stronger one, against the prediction of minimum-resource theory.[9] Under some conditions, he proposed, the chance of future success will override the distribution of resources. Chertkoff asked:

> What about three-way power struggles as they actually occur in our experience? Is it reasonable, for instance, to expect a coalition between the two weakest candidates at a political convention where the votes are divided so that $A>B>C$, $A<(B+C)$? . . . It may be that in such a situation the strongest in terms of number of votes will not be excluded from the winning alliance but will actually be the preferred coalition partner of both of the other candidates.

He continued:

> At the political convention, the candidate's probability of victory in the national election is of vital concern to the delegates, and it is usual, although not always the case, that the man with the most votes at the convention is the one with the best chance of winning the November election. If so, the most powerful in terms of number of votes may be the preferred choice of those seeking to form alliances.[10]

He tested the importance of the probability of future electoral success in an experiment using a simulated political convention. The subjects, 288 college students enrolled in an introductory psychology course at Iowa State, were divided into triads, with 24 triads playing in one of four different situations. In all four of the situations, player A had 40 delegate votes, B had 30, and C had 20. In three of the four situations, probable electoral success was added as a factor. B and C were given 50 percent chances of winning the election in all three situations, while A was given a 50 percent chance in one, a 70 percent chance in the second, and a 90 percent chance in the third. The fourth situation included no information on future electoral success.

Results indicated some support for the hypothesis. One finding from the study is summarized in Table 2.2. In the condition where no information about electoral chances was given, minimum coalition BC formed sig-

[9] Jerome Chertkoff, "The Effects of Probability of Future Success on Coalition Formation," *Journal of Experimental Social Psychology*, 2 (1966):265–77.
[10] Ibid., p. 266.

Table 2.2 Effects of Initial Resources and Future Success on Coalition Formation

CONDITIONS		NUMBER OF COALITIONS FORMED			
Delegate Votes A–B–C	Electoral Chance A–B–C	AB	AC	BC	chi square[a]
40–30–20	none given	1	9	14	10.75[b]
40–30–20	50%–50%–50%	6	8	10	1.00
40–30–20	70%–50%–50%	8	8	8	0.00
40–30–20	90%–50%–50%	10	10	4	3.00

[a]chi square based on two degrees of freedom
[b]significant at .01 level

Source: Jerome Chertkoff, "The Effects of Probability of Future Success on Coalition Formation," *Journal of Experimental Social Psychology* 2 (1966):271. Reprinted by permission.

nificantly more often than other coalitions. This effect evaporated, however, when the electoral probabilities were added. The numbers of delegate votes no longer predicted the outcomes. Adding electoral success changed the results (compare the first row of the table with the last three rows). BC coalitions decreased and AB coalitions increased as A's electoral chances went from 50 to 70 to 90 percent probabilities of success, although these results do not achieve statistical significance. As A's electoral chances improved, A became more likely to be included in a winning coalition.

GAME-THEORETIC STUDIES

A second stream of coalition research, more familiar to political scientists, is the mathematical game-theoretic literature. This developed from von Neumann and Morgenstern's work published in 1944[11] and is perhaps best known to political scientists through Riker's work with the size principle.

This approach is *theoretical*, but *nonempirical*. Game theory is not concerned with describing or explaining actual coalition behavior but with elaborating the formal, logical relationships that would hold in a given situation. R. D. Luce and H. Raiffa cautioned:

> It is crucial that social scientists recognize that game theory is not *descriptive* but rather (conditionally) *normative*. It states neither how people do

[11] J. von Neumann and O. Morgenstern, *Theory of Games and Economic Behavior* (Princeton, N.J.: Princeton University Press, 1944).

behave nor how they should behave in an absolute sense, but how they should behave if they wish to achieve certain ends. (italics in original)[12]

The direct contrast with Gamson's account of descriptive theory should be clear. This does not mean, however, that game theory is incapable of making empirical assertions (as will be seen in Chapter 3). Most practitioners would say that the theory can have important empirical applications.

Central to game theory is the assumption of rationality: players are considered rational when they apply the best available means to achieve their ends, whatever those ends may be—whether "good," "bad" or "irrational." They try to maximize their returns or minimize their losses from the situation. Also central to game theory is the calculation of what others in the game can be expected to do. Game theory, then, is the formal study of the rational, reciprocal expectations that players can make about each other's behavior. Such a study can be applied to players in any situation—bridge, poker, simple two-person games, coalition situations, or war.[13]

The name *game theory* arose originally from the observation that many problems of strategy can be formally treated as if they were games. One can designate a set of players, rules, and strategies, and make assumptions about rationality and interdependence. Players in chess, bridge, or poker select strategies to maximize returns and minimize losses. The best move depends on what one's opponent (or partner) is expected to do, and the problem of selecting the best strategy can be subjected to formal, logical analysis.

All games have a common set of characteristics. They consist of *players*, with *resources* and *goals*: the poker player with money, the nation with weapons, the legislative faction with a bloc of votes. They consist also of a *set of rules* specifying what the players can and cannot do and the procedure for the game. Some rules are clearly set forth, as in the moves of the pieces in chess; others, as in international diplomacy, are much more complex and ambiguous. The rules specify also the outcomes of the game—what game theory calls the *payoffs* to the player. Rational players will calculate the best ways to achieve their goals, given the rules and their own resources and taking into account the other players' calculations. The alternative actions thus calculated are called *strategies*. For each player, and each strategy, a *payoff matrix* can be derived: that is, the payoff each player would receive if the strategy is followed. If player A follows a strategy permitting winning five

---

[12] R. Duncan Luce and H. Raiffa, *Games and Decisions* (New York: John Wiley, 1957), p. 63. For a concise statement of the difference between the two coalition approaches, see William Gamson, "A Theory of Coalition Formation," *American Sociological Review* 26 (June 1961):380.

[13] Note that these assumptions can be applied to all coalition research. We assumed in Chapter 1 that players seek to maximize their own returns from the situation and are conscious of other similarly rational players. Game theory simply clarifies and formalizes these common assumptions.

dollars from B, the payoff matrix for that strategy would be noted as ($+5$, -5). A strategy where both would break even would be noted as (0, 0).

Rational players must calculate others' strategies as well as their own, and must assume that the others are doing the same for them. Even in a very simple situation—say, with only two players each with only three choices of action—this calculation can become exceedingly complex. Game theory provides a way of analyzing this complexity—of showing the best possible strategy for each player assuming both players play the best they can.

The major technique of game theory is *mathematical*. Mathematics is singularly suited to the study of formal and logical relationships and to the complexity of the calculations required. A simple two-person game might be diagrammed out on a sheet of paper, but as one begins to add players, various sets of preferences, and all possible combinations of results, the problem soon becomes unmanageable except through mathematical calculations. Martin Shubik calculated a general formula for n players as giving $2^n - 1$ possible coalition results, in a situation in which each player must only decide to join or not to join with every other player.[14] Note how rapidly the number of possible outcomes increases as one adds players—even in this very limited game:

Number of players	Number of outcomes possible
2	3
3	7
4	15
5	31
10	1023
20	more than 10^6

The problems, or games, of game theory range from two-person to n-person (n meaning any number larger than two), and those whose payoff is either zero-sum or non-zero-sum. In zero-sum games, the gains and losses of the players cancel each other: what some players win others lose. In non-zero-sum games, the gains and losses do not cancel: all or some players can gain, or all or some can lose.[15] We can first illustrate the uses of game theory for some two-person games and then turn to the n-person case. The

---

[14] Martin Shubik, "The Uses of Game Theory," in *Contemporary Political Analysis*, ed. James Charlesworth (New York: Free Press, 1967), p. 249.

[15] Games can also be categorized as constant-sum or non-constant-sum (also called variable sum). In constant-sum games, the sum of the payoffs to all players is equal to some constant (for example, 100 or -100) or zero. In non-constant-sum games, the sum of the payoffs varies according to the strategy choices of the players. Note that all constant-sum games are like zero-sum games in their solutions. The difference is that both or all players can win (or lose) something.

problem of *n*-person games, critical to the study of coalition behavior, requires some additional explanation.

Imagine players A and B, with opposing interests, faced with a decision among three choices, with the payoff matrix given below. (Since the interests are opposed, only A's payoffs are given in the matrix. B's are the reverse, or the opposite sign, of A's values: for example, A's -10 is B's $+10$.) A will select a whole row of chances, B will select an entire column. They will make their choices known to each other at the same time, and the payoff will be the number at the intersection of row and column. This is a two-person zero-sum game.

		Player B		
		b_1	b_2	b_3
	a_1	8	-5	-10
Player A	a_2	0	-2	6
	a_3	4	-1	5

At first, A might be tempted to choose strategy a_1 because his largest payoff (8) is found there; and B might be tempted to choose b_3 because her largest payoff (10) is there. But if A is rational and B assumes A is rational, B would not choose b_3, nor would A choose a_1. If A played a_1, B could play either b_2 or b_3, and A would be beaten badly. If B played b_3, A could play either a_2 or a_3, and B would be beaten badly.

But since both must calculate the best they can do given the other person's simultaneous calculation, A should decide on a_3 and B on b_2. Therefore (a_3, b_2) is the best outcome and the "solution" to the game. We say that a game with such a solution has a *saddle point*: an entry in the game matrix that is the smallest in its row and the largest in its column—in other words, it is the best that can be done in the situation. In the example, (a_3, b_2) is the saddle point. (Note that there can be only one saddle point.)

For this and other situations, game theory analyzes the best solutions for an individual, given the possible strategies of others, and determines whether there exists a stable and best solution for the players as a whole.

The above game permitted each player only one action. Imagine the same two players with opposing interests in a game with three moves. Each player, again, assumes the other is calculating the strategies for both. Such a two-person, three-step game is still exceedingly simple, compared to most problems of strategy faced in the real world. Nevertheless, the great increase in complexity as we add moves or players should be apparent.

Player A moves first and has two choices: 1 or 2. B can then choose 1,

Figure 2.2   Game Tree for a Two-Person, Three-Step Game

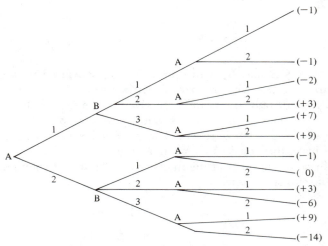

(−1)
(−1)
(−2)
(+3)
(+7)
(+9)
(−1)
(0)
(+3)
(−6)
(+9)
(−14)

Source: Anatol Rapoport, *Fights, Games, and Debates* (Ann Arbor, Mich.: University of Michigan, 1960), p. 141. © 1960 by the University of Michigan.

2, or 3, at which point A can choose 1 or 2 and the game is over. There are 12 different possible outcomes ($2 \times 3 \times 2 = 12$), and the game can be diagramed as in Figure 2.2. The diagram (called a game tree) shows all the possible moves and their final outcomes with payoff values. The letters indicate whose move it is and the numbers on the branches the choices available on that move. The numbers in parenthesis at the end of the game tree show the payoffs to A. (The payoffs to B are the same numbers with the opposite sign.)

In this apparently simple game, A has a total of 16 strategies and B has 9, and the full game matrix will have $16 \times 9 = 144$ entries. (See Figure 2.3.) The matrix shows a saddle point at $a_{12}b_1$. A payoff of 0 to both players is the best they can do in the situation. The value of this kind of analysis should be clear. The game "collapses" to a solution that both players can recognize, and *the outcomes can be known before the game is played.* In this case, of course, with payoffs of 0, players A and B might as well skip the game entirely. With a different payoff matrix, for example one with a saddle point of -1, A and B could also skip the game if A simply paid B the 1 unit value.

Game theory can also analyze situations of more complexity, in which probabilities have to be calculated because of uncertain information, and in which mixtures of strategies can be derived. For example, player A may have a preferred strategy only as long as B cannot be sure A will play it: therefore, A must calculate the best ratio of times of playing the preferred strategy compared to other strategies.

Figure 2.3   Payoff Matrix for a Two-Person, Three-Step Game

	b_1	b_2	b_3	b_4	b_5	b_6	b_7	b_8	b_9
a_1	-1	-1	-1	-2	-2	-2	-7	-7	-7
a_2	-1	-1	-1	-2	-2	-2	9	9	9
a_3	-1	-1	-1	3	3	3	7	7	7
a_4	-1	-1	-1	-2	-2	-2	7	7	7
a_5	-1	-1	-1	3	3	3	7	7	7
a_6	-1	-1	-1	-2	-2	-2	9	9	9
a_7	-1	-1	-1	3	3	3	9	9	9
a_8	-1	-1	-1	3	3	3	9	9	9
a_9	-1	3	9	-1	3	9	-1	3	9
a_{10}	-1	3	-14	-1	3	-14	-1	3	-14
a_{11}	-1	-6	9	-1	-6	9	-1	-6	9
a_{12}	0	3	9	0	3	9	0	3	9
a_{13}	0	-6	9	0	-6	9	0	-6	9
a_{14}	0	3	-14	0	3	-14	0	3	-14
a_{15}	-1	-6	-14	-1	-6	-14	-1	-6	-14
a_{16}	0	-6	-14	0	-6	-14	0	-6	-14

Source: Anatol Rapoport, *Fights, Games and Debates* (Ann Arbor: University of Michigan, 1960), p. 145.© 1960 by the University of Michigan.

N-Person Games

Since a coalition situation requires three or more players and an opportunity for cooperation, it is the *n*-person game that will be useful to coalition analysis—and in particular, the type of *n*-person game that permits a cooperative solution. In a game with *n* players and all conceivable coalitions possible, *n*-person game theory asks (1) which coalitions will actually form or are least likely to form and (2) how the collective payoff of a coalition will be apportioned among its members.

Consider the following three-person game, in which players are instructed to divide a dollar between them, the division to be determined by majority vote. Any two people with a majority can form a coalition and exclude the third player if they agree on how the dollar should be divided. The *characteristic function* of the game—a listing of the potential value commanded by each of the possible coalitions—is given below:

Coalition	Value
A	0
B	0
C	0
AB	$1
AC	$1
BC	$1
ABC	$1

Put more formally, an *n*-person game in characteristic-function form is defined by naming all the possible nonempty subsets of the *n* players in the game, and assigning a real number value to each subset. The value represents the utility commanded by that subset in coalition against all the other players.

Each single player forms a minority and therefore commands nothing. Each pair is a majority and commands the payoff of $1. The "grand coalition" of ABC also commands $1, but there would be little incentive for any two players to help form it, since they would have to divide the payoff three ways instead of two.

In many two-person games, players can calculate mathematically the solution that represents the best they could do given the other person's simultaneous calculation. When we move, however, from two to *n* players, our problems increase dramatically. In *n*-person games, the solutions are indeterminate—there may be no one solution or an infinite number. In the example above, we can reason from the characteristic function that either an AB, AC, or BC coalition will form, but we cannot say which nor can we say what the division of the dollar will be.

Nevertheless, it is possible to narrow the range of likely solutions for *n*-person games. *N*-person game theorists define an *imputation* as a particular split of the total payoff among the players in which (1) everyone does at least as well as he or she would have done by entering no coalition and (2) the value to the coalition as a whole is realized.[16] The solutions, in short, will be limited to those results that appear rational for the individual and the group as a whole to pursue. Game theorists then can apply solution concepts that specify what additional properties a set of imputations would need to qualify as a solution (i.e., what additional assumptions can be made about what the players can be expected to do). Solution concepts now being used by political scientists include the "core," the "kernel," the "bargaining set," and the "competitive solution," as well as applications of the Shapley-Shubik power index.[17] The subject, however, is still very much under development and evaluation.

The range of possible solutions can be narrowed still further by intro-

[16] See von Neumann and Morgenstern, *Theory of Games and Economic Behavior*.

[17] For summary, see Anatol Rapoport, *N-Person Game Theory* (Ann Arbor, Mich.: University of Michigan Press, 1970), and Morton Davis, *Game Theory: A Nontechnical Introduction* (New York: Basic Books, 1973), pp. 134–98. See also L. S. Shapley and Martin Shubik, "A Method of Evaluating the Distribution of Power in a Committee System," *American Political Science Review*, 48 (September 1954): 787–92; R. J. Aumann and Michael Maschler, "The Bargaining Set for Cooperative Games," in *Advances in Game Theory*, ed. M. Dresher et al. (Princeton, N.J.: Princeton University Press, 1964), pp. 443–76; M. A. Davis and M. Mascher, "The Kernel of a Cooperative Game," *Naval Research Logistics Quarterly* 12 (1965):223–59; Richard McKelvey et al., "The Competitive Solution for *N*-Person Games Without Transferable Utility, with an Application to Committee Games," *American Political Science Review* 72 (June 1978):599–615.

ducing additional assumptions—for example, constraints on bargaining or other rules of the game that may prevent some coalitions from forming. Many game-theory applications use such additional assumptions to achieve a finite, and often very specific, solution, at the same time that they increase the relevance of the analysis to real-world conditions. The problem with the indeterminacy of solutions for n-person games is, then, often circumvented in actual practice.

While many students of politics think of "coalition theory" as synonymous with "game theory," it should now be clear that that is not the case. Coalition theory includes studies (the social-psychological literature) that are not part of game theory nor derived from it, and game theory includes studies (all two-person games; some n-person games without mixed-motive situations) that do not involve coalition formation.

Studies of Coalition Behavior

While much of game theory by political scientists has concentrated on the two-person game, there has been some interesting application to the study of coalitions. A famous early study, by R. Duncan Luce and Arnold Rogow, analyzed legislation in Congress as a case of a three-person game consisting of the two congressional parties and the President.[18] Luce and Rogow derived thirty-six possible outcomes from their model and a number of conclusions about when the President or either party will be strong or weak. Most of their conclusions, however, can be reached without game theory by standard observations of American government: for example, that a minority party will need the President's support; or that a President can be strong when the two parties are deadlocked, with some members of each party defecting to the other side. William Riker used game theory to develop the *size principle*. Riker argued that for zero-sum games with perfect information, coalitions will form only to the point at which they reach minimum winning size. Beyond that point, there will be no incentive for members of coalitions to add more members. This conclusion, which is important and not obvious in its political implications, has been widely adopted and tested.

These two classic works remain the most frequently cited to illustrate game theory's value for the study of coalitions.[19] More recent studies have applied game theory to a range of political subjects that include cabinet co-

---

[18] R. Duncan Luce and Arnold Rogow, "A Game Theoretic Analysis of Congressional Power Distributions for a Stable Two-Party System," *Behavioral Science*, 1 (April 1956): 83–95.

[19] See, for example, Steven Brams, *Game Theory and Politics* (New York: Free Press, 1975). One chapter of seven is devoted to "Coalition Games" and much of that chapter to the Luce and Rogow and Riker models. Other chapters address two-person international games and studies of voting, vote-trading, and elections.

alition formation,[20] international alliances,[21] and legislative decisions.[22] Other work has attempted to extend the kind of processes that can be treated mathematically, such as games with cooperative solutions, with imperfect information on the part of the players, and with greater range of bargaining options possible.[23] The McKelvey et al. solution for n-person cooperative games performs well in predicting real-world coalitions.[24] Other solutions for cooperative games are also being proposed. In all of these cases, writers are extending the uses of game theory to confront problems common to coalition formation.

Example: Game Theory and a Political Convention

Steven Brams and Jose Garriga-Pico applied game theory to analyze bandwagons in coalition formation.[25] They sought to determine, for large voting bodies approaching infinite size, the point at which uncommitted delegates might most successfully support candidates for a political nomination. They assumed that uncommitted members wish to maximize their returns in joining a coalition, and that they therefore wish to join a minimum winning coalition. They stipulated further—among other assumptions—that two candidates and their supporters (blocs X and Y) compete for uncommitted delegate support, with a simple majority rule deciding the nomination.

The development of the mathematical logic can be paraphrased as follows. The authors calculated the probability that X or Y was the faster-growing bloc and would become minimum winning, and thus showed the expected utility for delegates choosing either. From this equation, they demonstrated how delegates can calculate their utility knowing only the size of the two blocs at any one stage in the process. The authors went on to derive the probabilistic contribution of an uncommitted member to any potential coalition. It is equal to how much the delegate, by joining a faster-

[20] See, for example, Abram DeSwaan, *Coalition Theories and Cabinet Formation* (San Francisco: Jossey-Bass, 1974); and Robert Axelrod, *Conflict of Interest: A Theory of Divergent Goals with Applications to Politics* (Chicago: Markham, 1970).

[21] See Mancur Olson, Jr. and Richard Zeckhauser, "An Economic Theory of Alliances," in *Economic Theories of International Politics*, ed. Bruce Russett (Chicago: Markham, 1968), pp. 24–25. See also Francis Beer, *The Political Economy of Alliances* (Beverly Hills and London: Sage Publications, 1972).

[22] See Barry Weingast, "A Rational Choice Perspective on Congressional Norms," *American Journal of Political Science* 23 (May 1979):245–62; and Kenneth Shepsle, "Institutional Arrangements and Equilibrium in Multidimensional Voting Models," *American Journal of Political Science* 23 (February 1979):25–59.

[23] One compilation of some of this newer work can be found in Peter Ordeshook, ed., *Game Theory and Political Science* (New York: New York University Press, 1978).

[24] McKelvey et al., "The Competitive Solution for N-Person Games"

[25] Steven Brams and Jose Garriga-Pico, "Bandwagons in Coalition Formation," *American Behavioral Scientist* 18 (March/April 1975), 472–96. This article is part of a series of studies by Brams, Riker, and several co-authors. See bibliography.

growing bloc X, would contribute to the probability that X eventually became a minimum winning coalition. Finally, they showed the "share of spoils," or payoffs, a delegate might expect to receive, depending on that contribution. The authors commented:

> We in effect assume that uncommitted members, acting rationally, do not simply join a [potential coalition] when it achieves its greatest chance of victory, or when they can make the largest probabilistic contribution and presumably derive the greatest benefits. Instead, we assume that they join when the combination of "winningness" and "benefits" on the average promises them the greatest spoils.[26]

These calculations led to the development of a "two-thirds" rule for successful bandwagon-joining. Given uncertainties and the fact that the uncommitted delegates' estimate of which is the faster-growing bloc will be correct two-thirds of the time (on the average), the best time to join one potential coalition is when it enjoys a 2:1 probabilistic edge over the other— when it is perceived roughly to be a 2:1 favorite to win. This may occur when blocs have few or many members: joining "early" or "late" may be equally valuable as long as the 2:1 ratio holds.

This result holds only within the limits of the model. The existence of more than two blocs (more than two serious candidates in the race), delegate defections or shifts, joining more-than-minimum-winning coalitions, among other possibilities, would change the results. Nevertheless, the work shows how this kind of analysis can be applied to an important political question. The analysis could be extended to other strategic situations.

EMPIRICAL POLITICAL STUDIES

Research in this area can be summarized more briefly than the other two approaches. It is more familiar to political scientists, needs less detailed explanation, and is itself less fully developed. Its importance, however, is at least equal to that of the other approaches in suggesting future coalition research.

The empirical studies seek to explain a political phenomenon, whether an event (a government overthrow), a process (the way in which cabinet seats are assigned), or a relationship (the conditions under which minor powers form coalitions with major powers in an international system). The explanation and the political effect are central, with coalition analysis used insofar as it contributes to this explanatory goal. These empirical political studies are like the social-psychological studies in that they seek to explain how coalition players actually behave in the real world under a variety of

[26] Ibid.

conditions. They are unlike them in using the concerns and techniques of the political science discipline; and unlike them, too, in showing less interest in developing an empirical theory of coalitions. What theory has been used has been borrowed from game theory; the social-psychological literature has not been utilized. The emphasis, then, may be characterized as *empirical* and *political*.

These studies, reflecting empirical political science generally, are wide-ranging and eclectic in technique. Depending on the subject matter and the researcher's design, they include descriptive case studies, careful analysis of small numbers of cases, or sophisticated quantitative designs. The uses of this approach for the study of coalitions can perhaps best be shown by subject matter category, as in the following section.

Studies of Coalition Behavior

We should first exclude the number of studies that use the word *coalition* loosely to mean merely an aggregate, or collection, of separate political components. People speak of a candidate's "electoral coalition" or "ideological coalitions" when they mean merely groups that have found themselves, or have been arranged to be found, together. There is no consciousness on the group's part that they are involved in coalition formation, and at times not even consciousness of themselves as a group. By the definition given in Chapter 1, we restrict coalition studies to those in which actors join together to determine outcomes in mixed-motive situations: the actors are aware of themselves as actors in such a situation, of their mix of motives, and of their opportunity to determine a political result. We thus exclude a number of political studies.

One major area of political coalition research has concerned cabinet coalition formation. In parliamentary democracies consisting of more than two parties, no one party alone may dominate the legislature and control the government. The parties, considered as the coalition actors, are faced with the problem of forming coalitions to organize the government and allot the cabinet posts. This important and frequently occurring political problem has been the subject of much research. Many writers have analyzed cabinet coalition formation for individual countries.[27] Eric Browne and others have studied coalition formation across a number of nations, and the quantitative

---

[27] See, for example, the various "Cases from Four Continents," in *The Study of Coalition Behavior*, ed. Sven Groennings et al. (New York: Holt, Rinehart and Winston, 1970), pp. 9–250. See also Eric Damgaard, "Party Coalitions in Danish Law-Making, 1953–1970," *European Journal of Political Research* 1 (1973):35–66; D. Wood and J. Pitzer, "Parties, Coalitions, and Cleavages: A Comparison of Two Legislatures in Two French Republics," *Legislative Studies Quarterly* (May 1979):197–226; and W. P. Y. Ting, "Coalition Behavior Among the Chinese Military Elite," *American Political Science Review* (June 1979):478–93.

and qualitative awarding of cabinet posts.[28] Lawrence Dodd, also using a comparative multi-nation approach, has examined the relationship between the kind of coalition formed and the stability of the cabinet government. Coalitions are classified as minimum-winning, more than minimum-winning, and less than winning, and so the size of the coalition is tested for its effect on the duration of the government.[29]

Taken together, the studies illustrate the possibilities for empirical work on coalitions. They comprise a large and well-developed area of research. The particular problem of coalition formation is intuitively obvious and so are the coalitions formed. The political subject is important and accessible to analysis, and the results tell us much of the theory and practice of cabinet formation.

Another major area of empirical research concerns unique and critical events, often marking a historic turn in a government or a policy. The American Constitutional Convention, the Civil Rights movement, changes in the government in Germany, and the South's defection prior to the Civil War have all been studied.[30] John Kessel supplied a major analysis of the Goldwater coalition,[31] and John Manley a study—with interviews from some participants themselves—of the conservative coalition in Congress.[32] We can thus identify for any one momentous occasion the coalition actors and the processes of coalition formation. We can explain the event, and perhaps generate hypotheses for other events, by the use of coalition analysis.

A third, more recently emerging research area concerns presidential nominations. Taking the convention delegates as coalition players, studies show the importance of a candidate's initial resources, momentum, and ideological position, and examine the effects of various rule changes.[33] A study by John Aldrich looked at the candidates as players and pointed out that even though the single-winner outcome of a nomination discourages coalition formation among candidates, temporary coalitions between them can

---

[28] Eric Browne, "Aspects of Coalition Payoffs in European Parliamentary Democracies," *American Political Science Review* 67 (June 1973):453–69, and "Qualitative Dimensions of Coalition Payoffs," *American Behavioral Scientist* 18 (March/April 1975):530–56.

[29] Lawrence Dodd, *Coalitions in Parliamentary Government* (Princeton, N.J.: Princeton University Press, 1976).

[30] See the examples in Groennings et al., *The Study of Coalition Behavior*.

[31] John Kessel, *The Goldwater Coalition* (Indianapolis, Ind.: Bobbs-Merrill, 1968).

[32] John Manley, "The Conservative Coalition in Congress," *American Behavioral Scientist* 17 (November/December 1973):223–47.

[33] See Eugene McGrevor, Jr., "Uncertainty and National Nominating Coalitions," *Journal of Politics* 40 (November 1978):1011–42; Larry Gerston et al., "Presidential Nominations and Coalition Theory," *American Politics Quarterly* 7 (April 1979):175–97; James Zais and John Kessel, "A Theory of Presidential Nominations with a 1968 Illustration," in *Perspectives on Presidential Selection*, ed. Donald Matthews (Washington, D. C.: Brookings, 1973), pp. 120–42; and Barbara Hinckley, "The Initially Strongest Player: Coalition Games and Presidential Nominations," *American Behavioral Scientist* 18 (March/April 1975):497–512.

occur. This can be seen in their decisions to enter or not enter primaries, which he documented with a number of instances of temporary stop-the-frontrunner coalitions.[34]

Other studies have looked at legislative decisions and international relations, among other subject areas. While many of these studies employ a large number of cases, few of them cross subject matter areas for any broader generalizations—other than references, of course, to the size principle. The following example, however, is an attempt to link a specific political subject—presidential nominations—with such broader generalizations.

Example: An Empirical Political Study and a Political Convention

One study examined the conditions advantaging or disadvantaging the initially strongest player in presidential nominating situations: that is, when, in a situation $A>B>C$, $A<B+C$, player A will be included in the winning coalition.[35] The size principle predicts that in zero-sum situations, given full information, A would be excluded and minimum-winning coalition BC would form. Minimum-resource theory makes the same prediction. But since political conventions are characterized by uncertainty and confusion, in which the candidates remain uncertain about shifts in delegate strength, uncertainty may lead to a situation (predicted by Gamson) of random choice: player A is equally likely to be chosen or not chosen. Or it may lead to a self-fulfilling prophecy whereby the candidate who appears to be the most likely to win gains additional support and does go on to win the nomination: thus player A would be included in the winning coalition. Finally, Chertkoff predicted that indicators of future electoral success, not of present nominating success, will influence whether A is or is not included.

Presidential nominations by the two major political parties were examined for the post World War II historical period. Measures were constructed for the candidates' initial strength, for the probability of nominating success (as indicated by having won in a convention situation before), and for the probability of electoral success by measures of public opinion polls and primaries.

Results of the study, reported in Table 2.3, show the likelihood against chance of various candidates being included in the winning coalition (in this case, winning the nomination). The initially strongest players, both the front-runners in the initial balloting and the perceived front-runners before the balloting, are significantly advantaged, as are some candidates distinctive in being past convention winners. The measures of probable electoral success are not significantly different from chance in their effects. The re-

[34] John Aldrich, *Before the Convention* (Chicago: University of Chicago Press, 1980), esp. pp. 157–61.
[35] Hinckley, "The Initially Strongest Player."

Table 2.3   Candidate Characteristics and Chance of Nomination Success

PROBABILITY OF NOMINATING SUCCESS	Win	Lose	N	Probability[a]
Frontrunners (first ballot)	8	1	9	.02*
Frontrunners (before balloting)	6	0	6	.02*
All past nominees	5	6	11	.50
Single past nominees	5	1	6	.11
Declared single past nominees	5	1	6	.11
Single past nominees who declared by the primaries	5	0	5	.03*
PROBABILITY OF ELECTORAL SUCCESS				
Preconvention poll leaders	6	3	9	.25
Primary winners	4	2	6	.34
Primary winners (alternate measure)	8	3	11	.11
Election losers	3	3	6	.66
Declared election losers	3	1	4	—

[a] The probability of obtaining the results by chance, under the binomial distribution for N's of 5 to 25. To specify the probability, we take the nominating results to be a sample of some hypothetical population of all possible nominations.
* Significant at .05 level.

Source: Barbara Hinckley, "The Initially Strongest Player: Coalition Games and Presidential Nominations," *American Behavioral Scientist* 18 (March/April 1975): 509. Reprinted by permission of the publisher, Sage Publications, Inc.

sults, within the limits of the study, support the prediction of a self-fulfilling prophecy advantaging the initially strongest player and argue against the other three predictions: of minimum resources, random choice, and future electoral success.

SUMMARY

The distinctions between these approaches should not be drawn too sharply. They merge at points in substance and within some of the same studies. Social-psychologist Gamson has analyzed presidential nominations. Cabinet coalition studies have used game theory, and several of the game theorists have used experiments. Studies of nominations by both John Aldrich and Steven Brams combined formal theory and empirical analysis.[36] Moreover, any one of these approaches can be usefully applied to the others—to generate hypotheses, test theories, or advance new formulations. Each can make a contribution to the study of coalitions and to each other. Students of nominations could correct many of those statements made about political conventions, and suggest, from their knowledge of the subject, alternative questions even more worthwhile as coalition research. The same holds for students of Congress and the Luce-Rogow model of legislative politics. The distinctions are not meant to oversimplify, but to clarify, the different primary concerns of the literature in each subject.

We find, then, the following somewhat ironic situation. We know that coalition analysis should be broadly applicable to the empirical study of politics, and yet much of the work to date has developed outside political science and is unfamiliar to it. Game theory appears best suited for analyzing simple political situations; so, while powerful, it is not necessarily of wide application. The empirical political studies have kept narrowly to subject matter boundaries and focused on important, often unique, events: accordingly, they have been able to develop and test few general statements about coalition behavior. Indeed, fascination with the size principle may substitute for such a development—leading people to think they have more "theory" than they do.

Nevertheless, we should now see that we are not limited to any one approach or specialization in the study of coalition behavior. Each may be pursued independently or used in combination. Results from one can raise questions for another. Ultimately, we might look forward to a closer merging of the three approaches and a firmer understanding of the limits and possibilities of each.

[36] Aldrich, *Before the Convention;* and Steven Brams, *The Presidential Election Game* (New Haven, Conn.: Yale University Press, 1978), esp. pp. 1–79.

Chapter 3

Problems of Analysis

Having examined the alternative approaches for the study of coalitions, we should now look at the problems associated with the various techniques. Each has its own limits and cautions to be recognized by the student of politics. Each, too, reflects some of the more general problems posed by empirical research. We are faced with the tension between simple and complex: between our models as "small measures" and the larger reality they model, between the simplicity of our measures and the complexity of political life. The world does not divide itself neatly into categories or stand still for our analysis. Politics is not Parcheesi. Experiments, formal theories, the study of actually occurring political events—all can be used in coalition research, but their problems should be recognized at the outset.

EXPERIMENTS

It is not surprising that students of politics have until recently largely ignored experimentation. Data from natural settings are widely available and compelling in their demand for explanation. Budgets are cut, presidential candidates nominated, cabinets formed, and ruling coalitions overthrown—frequently, under varying conditions, and with profound effect. Where events have such importance as to require explanation and such availability as to be studied directly, there is little incentive for indirect techniques.

A more serious deterrent to experimental work is the question of uniqueness—in political roles, setting, or stakes. If political actors and their environment are unusual, even unique, by definition, and if this uniqueness is thought to affect outcomes, only direct study may be appropriate. To take an extreme case, American presidents have been by ambition, background, and talent highly distinctive, their advisers in very different ways also unusual, and the circumstances—the White House, the sense of participation in history—virtually unique. Thus, while data on White House coalition formation are not widely available, serious questions can be raised about alternative experimental techniques. Even in less extreme cases, there remains the question of generalizing to political actors—by definition selected and self-selected by very special processes—from experimental subjects who are not similarly selected.

There may be uniqueness as well in the high stakes of some political situations. The stakes involve such things as capital punishment, war, and the making and breaking of careers and policies. Political stakes vary tremendously of course. However, unlike the closeness of the psychological experiment to analagous real-life situations, the highest-stake political games are not capable of simulation. Political science undergraduates in many ways constitute good experimental subjects. Competition for token points, small amounts of money, and grade points might simulate variation in stakes, although grade points, we assume, do not carry the intensity of war or capital punishment.

A key problem, then, for political scientists is *verisimilitude:* the likeness in certain critical respects to the political phenomenon being studied. It is related to a second problem of *validation*: namely, that we cannot ever prove to our complete satisfaction that the experiment simulates the essential feature of the relevant real-world situation. The laboratory and the laboratory subjects are, by definition, *not* the naturally occurring event we seek to explain.

Many phenomena, of course, can be considered independent of the effects of political role or stakes. Some will raise less concern with verisimilitude than others. Any design simplifies, and so distorts, naturally occurring phenomena, and the extent to which this distortion can be accepted is in part a matter of the researcher's judgment and in part an empirical question. When experimental results can be checked against, and applied successfully back to, naturally occurring results, we gain increased confidence in the technique.

On the positive side, the approach offers *control* by the researcher: the ability to select and manipulate the variables under study. Basically the procedure consists of studying the subject under highly controlled conditions, the control in major part designed and selected by the experimenter. The laboratory situation is artificial, created by the experimenter to provide the conditions required to study the phenomenon in question. These conditions may or may not be found in a nonlaboratory situation. As Paul Swingle pointed out, "the laboratory situation is not supposed to be a miniaturized or artificial replica of real-life situations but rather an experimental culture created and manipulated by the researcher."[1]

Requirements for the technique, as for any empirical inquiry, include appropriateness of the design to the questions under study, replicability, and what has been called "ecological validity,"[2] that is, appropriateness of generalization from the laboratory to the nonexperimental situation—what we have called verisimilitude. Also, researchers need to make sure that the subject is taking the measurement seriously. They need to consider if the experiment is interesting to the subject and, if deception is used, whether or not it is credible. A good experiment does not bore a subject unless boredom is a point of the experiment. And researchers need to prevent a subject from "cooperating"—consciously behaving in the manner that would be most useful to the experiment. Many subjects, it seems, want to contribute to the successful outcome of the experiment; they want to be "good subjects" and help validate the experimental hypothesis. Cover stories about the real purpose of the experiment are often employed to guard against such unhelpful cooperation.[3]

Certain other more specific requirements should also be mentioned. Standardization of the experimental conditions may be critical not only to guard against experimenter bias but also for replicability. Printed instructions or tapes are frequently used, and the physical environment should be the same for all runs. Instructions to the subjects, materials, and procedures should be fully reported. *Randomization* in assigning subjects to the various conditions is critical—each subject should have an equal chance of being assigned to any one of the experimental conditions. *Matching* the characteristics of the subjects and the control group to avoid possible extraneous effects is also critical. Swingle cited ages, sex, experimental naivete, time of year, IQ, and friendships among the possible contaminating factors.[4] Other factors, such as attitudinal or personality characteristics, might also need to be controlled by prior screening. Thus one might select same-sex subjects from a college population or a large undergraduate class, screening out possible relevant extraneous conditions and then randomizing the assignment of the matched subjects to the various conditions. A number of procedures are possible as long as the conditions of randomization and matching are met. Other, more specific, criteria for internal and external validity can also be cited.[5]

[1] Paul Swingle, ed. *Experiments in Social Psychology* (New York: Academic Press, 1968), p. 3.

[2] Egon Brunswik, *Systematic and Representative Design of Psychological Experiments with Results* (Berkeley: University of California Press, 1947).

[3] See Elliot Aronson and J. Merrill Carlsmith, "Experimentation in Social Psychology," in *The Handbook of Social Psychology*, 2nd ed., ed. Gardner Lindzey and Elliot Aronson (Reading, Mass.: Addison-Wesley, 1969), 2:54. Also see the full chapter summary, pp. 1–79.

[4] Swingle, *Social Psychology*, p. 3.

[5] Donald Campbell and Julian Stanley, *Experimental and Quasi-Experimental Designs for Research* (Chicago: Rand McNally, 1963).

To be successful at all, an experiment must be capable of *replication:* that is, others following the same procedure for the same kind of subjects should be able to produce the same results. One does not, therefore, design an experiment, gather one's subjects, and rush out to report the results. Unless the results can be reproduced, by oneself and others on further repetition, one has nothing of interest to say. Replication greatly reduces chance factors and any contamination by specific approaches, subjects, or settings, none of which ought to be measured within the experimental design. It is a minimally necessary condition for a successful experiment, although at times a very difficult one to achieve.

GAME THEORY AND POLITICAL APPLICATION

To discuss the problems of game theory in its political application, we need first recall the distinctive purpose of the approach. Game theory, like many other formal theories, is not centrally empirical in purpose: it seeks to explain not how people actually *do* behave, but how they *should* behave, under specified assumptions, if they are rational. Thus the primary purpose is not application or applicability. One has not "tested" one of its propositions in the real world unless the conditions and assumptions of the game are present.

For example, the size principle cannot be tested in natural political settings that do not pose (1) zero-sum situations, (2) strictly limited bargaining, and (3) perfect information; and few settings meet these conditions. All that we can say about the size principle is that it does or does not seem useful for an understanding of politics. We can do this by observing how often minimum winning coalitions form in the real world and the frequency of situations approximating these conditions.

A major problem, then, concerns the *usefulness* in real-world application. The conditions required for a game-theoretic analysis are often too strictly limited to apply to many political events. Like experiments, the conditions of a game formulation face the problem of verisimilitude in application to the political world.

Nevertheless, the problem should not be overstated. Political scientists, as opposed to mathematicians, presumably do not engage in mathematical exercises purely for their own sake. Game theorists themselves are concerned with the question of applicability, and, indeed, most of the practitioners in political science would hold that it is empirically useful. Minimum winning coalitions, said Riker, actually do form in the real world. Half of his book on the size principle was devoted to descriptive examples— from American history, political parties, and legislative coalitions—suggesting that this is the case. Many of the more recent studies include an experimental component for the purpose of testing the analysis against actually occurring behavior, and the results make clear that there are a number of situations in which people do behave as predicted.[6]

The following arguments are usually cited in support of the claim of political applicability. First, by analyzing games and classifying them by their rules and solutions, game theory contributes to an understanding of real-world games and how they fit in the classification. Second, by carefully specifying conditions under which certain results would hold, such as the rationality of players and the existence of perfect information, game theory supplies a base point for analyzing real world deviations. And finally, by expanding its own models to include more realistic conditions, such as poor information and probabilistic decisions, game theory is increasing its political applicability. In short, this rigorous, abstract thinking can clarify, and assist in the analysis of, the complexity of political life.

There is a second problem, however, for political scientists, and that is one of *communicability*. By and large, game theorists have not been able to communicate their ideas to a wider audience. In part, this is due to the general unfamiliarity with mathematical notation and argument. An essay, of direct relevance to the problem of lobbying in legislatures, begins as follows:

> Two lobbyists with equal budgets approach a legislature with the idea of buying votes. The lobbyists are on opposite sides of an issue: A wants the measure to pass, B wants it to fail. Lobbyist A offers amount x_i to voter i and B offers y_i, subject to the budget constraints $\Sigma x_i \leq a$ and $\Sigma y_i \leq b$ (a, b > 0), where the budgets are completely divisible. If $x_i > y_i$, then A controls voter i, if $y_i > x_i$, then B controls i, and if $x_i = y_i$, there is a standoff or "tie" for that voter. Let the set of votes be $N = \{1, 2, \ldots, n\}$, and the voting procedure be noted by collection $\bar{S}$ of winning sets. We assume, as usual, that $N \in \bar{S}$, $\phi \notin \bar{S}$, and $S \in \bar{S}$ and $S \subseteq T$ implies $T \in \bar{S}$. Then A wins (and B loses) if $\{i \in N : x_i > y_i\} \in \bar{S}$; similarly B wins (and A loses) if $\{i \in N : x_i \geq y_i\} \notin \bar{S}$.[7]

The writing is very clear and the mathematical notation quite straightforward—indeed, the example was selected for its clarity of presentation. Nevertheless, many political scientists interested in the problem of lobbying might well be discouraged by this first paragraph from reading further.

While part of the problem is unfamiliar notation, beyond this one finds little attempt to use *words* in the writing on game theory to translate the mathematical meaning. Where one can't understand, one can't criticize, and

---

[6] See, for example, Richard McKelvey et al., "The Competitive Solution for *N*-Person Games Without Transferable Utility, With an Application to Committee Games," *American Political Science Review* 72 (June 1978):599–615; Morris Fiorina and Charles Plott, "Committee Decisions under Majority Rule: An Experimental Study," *American Political Science Review* 72 (June 1978):575–98; and Peter Ordeshook, ed., *Game Theory and Political Science* (New York: New York University Press, 1978), pp. 215–356.

[7] H. P. Young, "A Tactical Lobbying Game," in Ordeshook, *Game Theory*, pp. 391–404.

so both the strengths and weaknesses of any game-theoretic work remain unappreciated by the large majority of political scientists. The result is a situation in which a small group of people are talking enthusiastically, in the language of mathematics, only to each other.

Some work has been done to bridge the gap between these disciplines. One excellent attempt was offered in a study by Abram DeSwaan, who sought to "test the claim that formal theories can explain important processes of political life," specifically, for "rational actors as they join in coalitions with or against one another."[8] In the first half of the book, DeSwaan outlined the major theories and their predictions for cabinet coalition formation, supplying mathematics and a translation for the nonmathematical reader. He included simplifying assumptions: that the coalition actor is the "parliamentary group" treated as a unanimous entity, with all internal disagreements ignored; that policy preferences can be reduced to a single dimension; that actors have no historical memory; and that events exist out of time. The remainder of the book is devoted to testing the theories with data on European cabinet formation, based on approximately 100 cases in which actors, resources, policies, and outcomes can be identified with some confidence. DeSwaan employed statistical analysis for his range of cases as well as explanations on a country-by-country and case-by-case basis. He concluded by questioning some of the original theories and modifying others on the basis of the empirical examination.

The advantages of the technique should be clear from the exposition in Chapter 2. Game theory offers a *logic and rigor* in analyzing political problems not so obviously available in other techniques. Moreover, it offers *solutions* for these problems, telling us the best that players may expect to do, acting rationally, in the situation. The outcomes can be analyzed before the game is played. Accordingly, rules or other restrictions leading to particular outcomes in actual practice can be reconsidered or revised. Finally, it offers a *classification* of political problems, in terms of their rules and solutions, that allows a large amount of very diverse phenomena to be organized within the theory.

COALITIONS IN NATURAL POLITICAL SETTINGS

The final technique we will examine, and the most familiar to political scientists, is the study of coalitions in natural political settings. We speak of "natural" as opposed to "artificial," the study of an actual event as opposed

[8] Abram DeSwaan, *Coalition Theories and Cabinet Formation* (San Francisco: Jossey-Bass, 1973), p. 1.

to the event created by the experimenter.[9] Both of these techniques require gathering and interpreting evidence, but the evidence from one is obtained from a designed laboratory experiment and the evidence from the other is obtained from events as they occur in political life. Indeed, the strong points of one technique are the problems of the other.

Experiments, we saw, raised the problem of verisimilitude and the advantage of control. In research in natural political settings, the opposite is the case. There is no problem with *verisimilitude*: the events are not only like those occurring in the real world, they are taken from that world. They are important, often compelling, in their demand for explanation. But there is a problem of *measurement* and *control*—of selecting out the factors we are particularly interested in studying from the whole flux and range of events. Unlike experiments, this kind of empirical political research finds its variables difficult to isolate and control. The selection and measurement of variables become major problems.

Three of the most critical problems facing the researcher can be dealt with at some length. One concerns the identification of a *coalition situation* from all the complex, multifaceted play of political events. A second concerns the identification of the *coalition actors* who could perceive themselves and others as involved in such a situation. A third concerns the assumptions that can be made about their *goals*, or motives, in the situation.

Coalition Situations

How do we recognize a coalition situation? What event do we look to and how can it be distinguished from other simultaneously occurring events? To what extent are we justified in defining after the fact that a coalition situation has occurred? The problem of identifying a coalition situation becomes the problem of defining the universe of cases for analysis.

Some political decisions involve no conflict and should be excluded by definition. Yet some purely consensual decisions may be afterproducts of earlier, less visible coalition activity. A unanimous resolution in a legislature or a Supreme Court decision may be the uninteresting afterproduct of an important though less visible earlier coalition process. Coalitions may form to prevent any disruptive and visible coalition situation or to avoid conflict and keep the trust between traditional partners. Identifying *after the fact* that there exists both conflict and coordination would exclude those less visible cases. We face the problem of eliminating either too much or too little.

---

[9] *Natural* is used in its dictionary meaning of "not artificial, synthetic, processed, acquired by external means." In this sense, natural settings are opposed to experimental artifice. Since *political* is also opposed to *natural* in the sense of "being or found in its native state" as, for example, a state of nature, it should be noted that only the former and not the latter meaning is here employed.

Coalition Players

A second problem concerns the definition of coalition players in real-world political settings: in particular, the choice between the individual as the unit of analysis or a larger bloc of individuals who can be assumed to have the same preferences. In some of the experimental models, autonomous individuals play orderly games. But in the real-world application—where some people have more influence than others, and where choices often have to be simplified or surrendered—the individual is not always the most useful or realistic choice for coalition actor. In many situations it is the attributes of groups (their number of members or other resources) that determine the bargaining and outcome. To work with blocs, however, requires additional assumptions of (1) consciousness on the part of the members of their own group identity and that of other groups, and (2) coordination and communication within and between blocs for purposes of bargaining and distributing rewards. The consciousness may be tacit or explicit, the communication more or less formal. One needs only to avoid analyzing decisions as outcomes of coalition activity when the actors were not aware of being in a coalition situation, or of their hypothetical partner's existence, or, as in the case of some collective constructs, even of their own existence.

A number of computer programs are designed to show the voting agreement over time of members of a legislature, court, or international assembly. One finds clusters, or blocs, of members who typically vote together. These programs, however, will not be useful for coalition analysis unless one can advance the independent argument that the conditions of consciousness and coordination are met.

While either individual or bloc would seem possible depending on the assumptions that can be made and the questions being asked, most applications to date have used the bloc as player. In some research, parties have been used for multiparty systems. In other research, factions in constitutional conventions. Gamson used "candidate blocs" for presidential nominations, with these blocks defined behaviorally by their vote for a presidential candidate on the first ballot. Others have used the state delegation.

Assumptions about Goals

The third critical problem concerns assumptions about goals—especially the equivalence of goals. Can we assume, for example, that actors seek to maximize their share of success from the situation? Particularly in low-stake situations, some actors may pursue goals outside the situation, such as visibility, experience, or psychic rewards. In multiple situations, succeeding at one point is often more important than succeeding at others. In all situations, winning is more important to some people than others. Assuming equivalence, then, as most studies do, introduces a considerable simplification of political reality. Whether or not it is justified must be left to the judgment of the researcher and readers of the work to determine.

Some of the problems of equivalence will be less severe than others depending on the particular research setting. If political actors are by definition concerned with power (that is, applying resources to determine outcomes), in most cases we can safely assume that winning is better than losing. In many cases, any single outcome can accommodate a wide range of individual goals. Further, while some decisions will indeed be more important than others, any individual nonequivalences should cancel each other when decisions are summed over time for all actors.

Members of Congress, for example, have been said to pursue three different major goals, depending on their personalities and the electoral situation: winning reelection, making good public policy, and gaining prestige in the institution.[10] A controversial decision, say on a farm bill, allows members to work for any of these goals. Members can work for reelection (working to win a crop subsidy for their constituents), or for policy purposes (believing that subsidies are good national policy), or they can work for power and prestige (caring little about subsidies, and knowing that their urban constituents also care little, they may vote with the side that is most likely to win—because in the pursuit of prestige and power, winning is more valuable than losing). We might find, then, on any one controversial subsidy decision that all members seek the policy that is the most favorable to them and that requires the least sacrifice. True, some decisions will be more important to some members than other decisions, but over time, all members can be assumed to face situations of great, moderate, and little importance.

MULTIPLE GOALS   In some situations, multiple goals can be specified for the coalition actors. One study proposed three distinct goals and predicted the various outcomes possible for three players, depending on which goal each pursued.[11] Assume that among players A, B, and C, resources are distributed so that A has more than B who has more than C, but both B and C together have more than A (A>B>C, A<B+C). These players may (1) seek *efficiency* of costs to coalition benefits by joining a minimum winning coalition, (2) seek *control* of the coalition by joining with a weaker partner, or (3) seek *security* for some other situation by joining the coalition with the largest total resources.

Given the situation described above, Player B can gain efficiency and control by choosing C and security by choosing A. Player C can gain efficiency by choosing B, security by choosing A, and cannot achieve control.

[10] Richard Fenno, *Congressmen in Committees* (Boston: Little, Brown, 1973).
[11] Bruce Bueno de Mesquita and Richard Niemi, "A Dynamic Theory of Coalition Formation" (Paper delivered at Midwest Political Science Association Meeting, Chicago, April 1980); see also Michael Taylor, "On the Theory of Government Coalition Formation," *British Journal of Political Science* 2 (July 1972): 361–73.

Player A seeks efficiency with C, security with B, and gets control either way. Altogether, there are twenty-seven different goal combinations that can predict the coalition outcome.[12] Thus, for example, if player A seeks security, player B control, and player C efficiency, a BC coalition is predicted. The goals are sufficiently general to apply to many political situations and can be employed in game theory or empirical analysis.

Some students of international relations have questioned the uses of coalition theory on the grounds that different nations may pursue different goals in the same international situation. Some nations may be seeking defense security, others the control of a particularly critical ally, and still others may be seeking the short-term efficiency of a minimum win. Moreover, nations will change goals as their domestic or foreign situation changes. However, this analysis suggests that alliances could be predicted formally or empirically by specifying the predominant goal that is being pursued.

In short, we need to avoid errors of inclusion or exclusion in identifying a universe of cases, to be careful in selecting the most appropriate unit of analysis, and to refrain from oversimplifying the motives of complex personalities when engaged in political situations. This should sound very familiar. While the problems should not be minimized, they appear no more severe than the usual problems of conceptualization and measurement faced in empirical political research. In many cases, they will merely reduce the power or precision of the explanation and so weight the results against whatever propositions are being tested.

These three problems must be faced in applying coalition analysis to natural political settings. Particular settings will raise additional problems of their own. Coalitions may be relatively easily analyzed when multiparty actors decide the awarding of cabinet posts, or nations divide territory in the wake of war. There are commonly perceived actors (parties, nations) who may be considered unitary and single purposed, and there are concrete measurable payoffs to be awarded. A discrete event has occurred; the "who gets what" can be directly observed. Other cases will be less conducive to direct translation: when activity involves many stages, and when the actors, situations, and returns are less easy to see.

SUMMARY

The tension of simple and complex that was identified at the beginning of the chapter can be seen throughout this discussion. Each of the three approaches raises its own problems. The simplifications of formal theories or experiments may be less than useful when applied to some political events, while the study of the events directly raises questions of identification and

---

[12] Bueno de Mesquita and Niemi, "Coalition Formation," p. 21.

control. If there are, as the next chapter suggests, at least twenty-three variables that must be isolated and interrelated, some carefully controlled designs will be necessary. Yet such controls can lead the study of "real world" coalitions back to mathematics and the experimental laboratory. Nevertheless, this tension is not unique to coalition research and should remain tolerable and capable of resolution.

If politics concerns applications of power in collective, mixed-motive situations, then the systematic study of such behavior is important. The results to date suggest that there are recurring patterns of behavior that can be identified, replicated, and generalized to other situations. Behavior identified under experimental conditions can be generalized to other settings; and political questions of interest can be analyzed mathematically and studied in the laboratory. Propositions from experiments or formal theories can be applied to natural settings and tested for usefulness and verisimilitude against the results of those cases. Results hypothesized from natural settings can be retested experimentally or reformulated mathematically. The list of variables in the following chapter invites the accumulation of natural studies while indicating questions requiring rigorous analysis and control. This is not to minimize the tension between simple and complex, but to suggest that all three approaches may be used with caution and used in combination.

II

EXTENSIONS

The first three chapters set forth the possibilities for studying coalitions and discussed the major approaches available. The focus now narrows to particular ways in which coalition analysis may become more useful in the study of politics. If coalitions for many political scientists mean single games and minimum-winning size, then the limited application in the past is not surprising. Accordingly, the following chapters extend the application. We can study coalitions beyond their winning size (Chapter 4), beyond the single game (Chapter 5), and beyond isolated events to the larger political environment (Chapter 6).

Chapter 4

Some Variables in the Study of Coalition Formation

We have examined a model and some approaches for applying coalitions to the study of politics. This chapter suggests a framework for the translation.[1] Given the gap between the claims and the performance of political coalition research, we need a mapping of the kind of analysis possible—one comprehensive enough to supply an overview and yet specific enough to use.

The list of variables presented in Table 4.1 offers one such preliminary mapping. All of the components on the list have been identified as important in coalition research. Most have been cited, although with differing emphasis, in the social-psychological studies, and some have been examined in the game-theoretic and empirical political studies. The table provides a single summary list of these various contributions. The chapter first translates the table into events and conditions of political interest and then sets forth its potential as a preliminary research schedule.

Several limitations should be noted at the outset. First, the table must be taken as provisional and preliminary, derived from research that is in the process of development. Items may be added as new research is undertaken, or they may be subdivided and combined. At present, some are defined more precisely than others. Second, the disadvantage of a table combining three approaches is that it may be intuitively attractive to no one. We will speak of variables—things that take a range of values and appear to influence or be influenced by other things as they do so. Still, it may seem awk-

---

[1] This chapter is a revised and expanded version of an article published by the author entitled "Twenty-One Variables Beyond the Size of Winning Coalitions," *Journal of Politics* 41 (February 1979): 192–212.

Table 4.1 Some Variables for the Study of Coalition Behavior

ATTRIBUTES OF ACTORS	INITIAL RESOURCE DISTRIBUTION	CONDITIONS AND RULES OF THE GAME		COALITION RESULTS
		Affecting the Situation	Affecting the Behavior	
1. Goals	8. Variation in initial resources	11. Number of players	15. Bargaining rules —open or closed —ease of communication —other specific rules	18. Choice of partner; kind of coalition formed
2. Attitudes toward winning and competition	9. Extent of one player's advantage	12. Stakes —size —positive or zero sum	16. Existence of positive or negative incentives	19. Coalition activity: some or no coalition forms
3. Experience with the game	10. Probability of success	13. Recurrence of the game	17. Information conditions —single vs. multiple vs. no clear cues —perfect or imperfect information	20. Coalition stability over time
4. Experience with the other players		14. Decision rules —for coalition —for outcome		21. Tendency to form conservative vs. revolutionary coalitions
5. Likeness or difference				22. Whether initially strongest player is included in a winning coalition
6. Status ordering				23. Distribution of returns or payoffs
7. Overlapping membership				

ward to game theorists to speak of the stakes of the game (as shown by a payoff matrix) as a variable *influencing* the outcome. They would say that knowing the stakes of the game and other rules allows us to *solve* for the outcome. The outcome is implicit in the definition of the game. At the same time, other questions might be raised by those who are not game theorists. For a final limitation, no set form or sequence is suggested by the organization of the table. It seemed preferable at this preliminary stage to leave relationships between components as open to interpretation as possible.

The major components of the coalition model are taken to be mixed-motive (1) actors with (2) an initial distribution of resources and (3) specified rules of the game engaged in (4) communication and bargaining with a view toward applying (5) resources to determine an outcome and distribute returns. (See Chapter 1.) The five columns of the table list variables relevant to these five major components; the many possible interrelationships are left open for future study.

One interpretation is implicit in the table and needs further attention. Coalition results, as the final column in the table, can be taken as the dependent variables—the "things to be explained." The other columns suggest independent variables—the influences affecting these results. Thus we could ask how variation in the size of stakes, number 12 in the table, will affect number 19—whether or not some sort of coalition will form. Stakes can vary from matters of life or death to token awards. So we are asking how changes in this independent variable will affect—or can help explain—the tendency for players to form coalitions or not. Depending on the questions asked, other arrangements of independent and dependent variables are possible. Coalition results can create new rules and resources for other situations and so might be the independent variables in some studies. One might study political feedback processes in which the rules, resources, and attributes of actors are maintained or transformed by coalition results—for example, a rule about bargaining might produce a political outcome that maintained or changed the rule. Therefore, the organization of the table, which lists coalition results and some influences on these results, is merely one of a number of possible interpretations.

The actors may be individuals or collectivities: nations engaged in diplomacy, parties voting on a tax measure, local interests seeking rezoning, staff members seeking influence with a chief executive. In short, they may be any set of political actors confronted with the need to determine outcomes in a collective mixed-motive situation.

DEPENDENT VARIABLES

We can begin by considering the column of coalition results—the effects we wish to explain. Of all of these, the *choice of coalition partner* (18) has received the most attention in both empirical and theoretical work. It specifies the particular kind of coalition formed among the actors—who joins with whom, who wins, and who loses. If coalitions determine outcomes of collective mixed-motive situations, the choice of partner determines which particular outcomes are formed. If A, B, and C are respectively, right, left, and center parties in a parliamentary system or three nations in a potentially explosive international situation, we ask the conditions under which AB, BC, or AC will form. In many cases, choice of partner is the single most important question, implicit in its outcome the policies of a government or the making of a war.

Bernhardt Lieberman analyzed the U.S.-Soviet nuclear test ban treaty of 1963 as the outcome of a three-person coalition situation:

> The treaty . . . can be and was seen by the Americans, Russians, and Chinese as similar to a single play of a three-person majority game . . . The U.S. and the Soviet Union formed an alliance on this issue, excluded the Chinese who were opposed to the test ban and concluded a treaty that appears to be mutually advantageous . . . When one adds the fact that if the Chinese agreed to the treaty, they probably could not develop an independent nuclear capability, the importance of the treaty to U.S.-Sino-Soviet relations is obvious.[2]

In Lieberman's analysis, the two nuclear powers A and B join in coalition to exclude C, replacing a communist coalition that had excluded the capitalist nation. That this change is perceived by China was nicely illustrated by a photograph Lieberman cited as having appeared in a Peking publication. The photograph showed the Communist leader Khrushchev hugging the American Secretary of State Harriman after the signing of the treaty, and the caption under the picture read "Khrushchev Embraces Capitalism."

Variable 18 is capable of a number of definitions. One may be interested in explaining under what conditions military equals will sign a treaty excluding nonequals, when center parties will join right-wing or left-wing parties, or when minimum winning or non-minimum winning coalitions will form. The size of winning coalitions, so heavily emphasized in previous coalition research, is merely one possibility indicated by this variable.

The *distribution of returns or payoffs* (23) is frequently studied along with choice of partner. In game theory, the payoff is the utility (or value) associated with the outcome of a game for a player or a coalition. Therefore, by knowing the choice of partner in game theory, we also know the payoff. In many experiments, too, a coalition is not acknowledged by the experimenter until the potential partners have agreed on the distribution of returns. In

---

[2] Bernhardt Lieberman, "The Sino-Soviet Pair: Coalition Behavior from 1921 to 1965," in *Sino-Soviet Relations and Arms Control*, ed. Morton Halperin (Cambridge, Mass.: M.I.T. Press, 1967), p. 326.

many cases, however, the choice of partner and the payoffs distributed to the partners are separately interesting questions. Recent political studies have examined payoffs for cabinet formation and for war coalitions.[3] A distribution may be proportionate to the resources that players bring to the coalition (parity) or it may follow from the perception that all players in the coalition are equally important to it and so should receive equal returns (equity). By parity, a player with twice as many resources as a potential partner would receive twice as large a share of returns. By equity, the player and potential partner would receive the same share of returns. Other less obviously "fair" distributions can also occur, varying with such factors as the players' attitudes toward competition, their experience with the game, and the clarity or confusion of the situation. Some people want even the losers to win something. Naive players may demand less—or more—than their fair share. Some situations are so confused that the resources cannot be firmly calculated: resources shift or are uncertain; players drop in or out of the game. Since the term *payoff* is particularly unfortunate for political discussion, one should note that returns can span the full range of political outcomes. They are the "what" of the "who gets what," including policies, ideological satisfaction, position, and more and less material rewards.

Political scientists have paid little attention to the other variables in this column. Yet these other coalition results have some obvious political importance.

Coalition activity (19) is a dichotomous variable that describes whether some or no coalitions form. It should be clear that the cases in which no coalitions form are as interesting as the cases in which they do. Many conditions make the choice *not* to choose a partner the best strategy for one or all participants. A player may prefer to remain inactive rather than disrupt a past trusted alliance. In some international situations, any coalition formed would lead to war; deciding not to form a coaliton avoids one. Some balance-of-power situations may be based on this mutual perception. Attack threatens a retaliatory coalition and may be deterred, in the interests of all parties, only as long as no coalition forms. Political scientists have speculated that nations in the same alliance will be "less free to compete with their allies in . . . spheres of incompatability and less free to cooperate with outsiders in areas of overlapping interests."[4] But this does not necessarily lead to the severely restricted situation in which partners, locked in coalitions,

[3] Eric Browne and Karen Ann Feste, "Qualitative Dimensions of Coalition Payoffs" *American Behavioral Scientist* 18 (March/April 1975): 92–118; Eric Browne and Mark Franklin, "Aspects of Coalition Payoffs in European Parliamentary Democracies" *American Political Science Review* 67 (June 1973): 453–569; and Abraham DeSwaan, *Coalition Theories and Cabinet Formation* (Amsterdam: Elsevier, 1973); Harvey Starr, *War Coalitions* (Lexington, Mass.: D. C. Heath, 1972).
[4] J. David Singer and Melvin Small, "Alliance Aggregation and the Onset of War, 1815–1945," in *Alliances*, ed. Francis A. Beer (New York: Holt, Rinehart and Winston, 1970), p. 16.

are forced into wars with nonpartners. Both partners and nonpartners can choose a no-coalition result.[5]

The other dependent variables concern key dynamics in the coalition-forming process. *Coalition stability* (20) measures the maintenance of a coalition over time, as in the frequency over time of a particular choice of partner. The political importance is obvious—for questions of political development, government stability, or kinds of policy change.[6] To ask whether *the player initially strongest in resources is included in a winning coalition* (22) is to ask about the ability to translate resources from one point in a political process to another. In conditions under which minimum winning coalitions form, strength paradoxically can become weakness and the initially strongest player may be excluded from the coalition. Other conditions produce the reverse; bandwagons roll when strength leads to further strength. The variable may be important, then, for analyzing presidential nomination politics, the effect of elections on subsequent coalition formation, or balance of power conditions in any situation.

The final variable to be considered is also concerned with translating resources from one point of distribution to another. The forming of *conservative versus revolutionary coalitions* (21) describes activity in a prescribed status order. The order may be social or political, with actors ranked by class, caste, socioeconomic status, bureaucratic hierarchy, constitutional form, seniority, or in some other way. A conservative coalition maintains the original status order, and a revolutionary coalition, by excluding the highest-status player, overturns it.[7] In a triad in which A has higher status than B, who in turn has higher status than C, AB is a conservative coalition, BC is a revolutionary coalition, and AC is neither conservative nor revolutionary. When President Truman found his Latin American foreign policy blocked by the "sugar subgovernment" of the Department of Agriculture, the House Agriculture Committee, and domestic sugar interests,[8] a revolutionary coalition could be said to have been formed that excluded the President as actor A. In another example, if we were to designate the House Democratic Party leadership of Congress (including its broad membership support) as actor A, the senior committee leaders as B, and the large class of Democratic freshman as C, then the 1975 overturn of senior chairmen in some committee posts could be seen as the forming of an AC coalition. Neither conservative nor revolutionary, it changed the outcome from a sixty-year-long conservative coalition in which A and B had joined forces to

---

[5] For some use of the "inactivity" or "indifference" concept by Singer and Small, see *The Wages of War: 1816–1965: A Statistical Handbook* (New York: John Wiley, 1972), pp. 342–45.

[6] For one study of stability in cabinet coalition formation, see Lawrence Dodd, *Coalitions in Parliamentary Government* (Princeton: Princeton University Press, 1976).

[7] *Two Against One: Coalitions in Triads* (Englewood Cliffs, N.J.: Prentice-Hall, 1968), pp. 50, 51.

[8] Douglas Cater, *Power in Washington* (New York: Random House, 1964), pp. 26–48.

maintain the seniority rule.[9] Or again, if A is a ruler, B a set of ministers, and C the army, the variable can describe the maintenance or overthrow of a government. In any application, the variable can describe how status resources allocated at one point are maintained or subverted at another point in the political process.

Questions of stability, revolution, maintenance, or the overthrow of an actor initially strongest in status or initial resources are worth explaining in their own right and are important for their wider impact in a political situation. Called dependent variables here, they could also be treated as independent variables, comprising factors affecting a range of other political (i.e., coalition) results. Coalitions may form to determine the outcome of rules and resources for later games. They may form to prevent a threat to a past satisfactory alliance. They may form to continue or terminate a coalition situation. If we are interested in the various feedback processes by which decisions maintain and reproduce similar decisions, then variables 21–23 can help to isolate key points in these dynamic processes.

INDEPENDENT VARIABLES

Coalition results include such things as government stability, revolution, redistribution of resources, and winning and losing. The first seventeen variables in the table point to conditions affecting these very important political events. *Variation in initial resources* (8) among the players has been the most frequently addressed. It is known to affect coalition behavior and results, and has been studied extensively in all three approaches. The variety of political resources was detailed in Chapter 1. If the resources are the number of members elected in a legislative faction, one is asking about the effect of elections in legislative coalition formation. The *extent of one player's advantage in resources* (9) suggests additional effects.[10] If the resources are delegates supporting a presidential candidate, at what point and under what conditions is the frontrunner able to forge a winning coalition? This question asks about the effect of variable 9 on variables 18 and 20. When one asks what rules or conditions help unanimous coalitions of all the weaker players to form against a resource leader,[11] one asks about the effect of variable 9 on variables 15, 16, and 17.

[9] Barbara Hinckley, "Seniority 1975: Old Theories Confront New Facts," *British Journal of Political Science* 6 (October 1976): 382–99.

[10] See James Phillips and Lawrence Nitz, "Social Contacts in a Three Person 'Political Convention' Situation," *Journal of Conflict Resolution* 12 (June 1968): 206–14.

[11] Abraham Horowitz and Amnon Rapoport, "Test of the Kernel and Two Bargaining Set Models in Four- and Five-Person Games," in *Game Theory as a Theory of Conflict Resolution*, ed. Anatol Rapoport, (Boston: D. Reidel, 1974), pp. 161–92; Pamela Oliver, "Selective Incentives in an Apex Game," *Journal of Conflict Resolution* 24 (March 1980): 113–41.

Probability of success (10) is a different kind of resource cue. When coalitions are formed in order to determine outcomes in a future—and very different—situation, the candidates' nominating chances may be affected by their probability of future election success. Do parties, considered as convention delegates assembled, actually want to win elections? In other words, how important is variable 10 in explaining the particular nominating coalition formed?

Jerome Chertkoff speculated:

> Perhaps in an intragroup squabble prior to inter-group conflict, participants in the intragroup squabble will prefer the strongest possible alliance, that is, the one which gives the group its best chance of victory against the opposition. Hence the alliance with the greatest probability of future success is preferred.[12]

Note how the word "squabble" trivializes the intragroup event compared to the intergroup "conflict." Many nominating situations, however, cannot be accurately characterized as squabbles. Clearly the effect of variable 10 and the conditions under which it may or may not have effect, in party nominations or other events, needs further investigation.

Those interested in empirical tests of democratic theory can see that the three variables just discussed can be determined by election results. Elections can provide the initial resource distribution, the extent of a player's advantage, and indications of future success. Public opinion polls do the same. So asking what effect initial resources have on any of the dependent variables—or the conditions under which they will not have effect—asks how a public input affects later coalition formation. If under some conditions the initially strongest player in the polls or in an election is not included in a winning coalition, one could argue that some perversion of the popular will has occurred. Coalitions determine outcomes in collective mixed-motive situations: hence the effect of initial resources compared against other effects may help trace democratic influence on government decisions.

Seen in this light, factors overriding initial resources are critically important. *Experience with the game* (3) and *experience with other players* (4) offer additional incentives and information.[13] The next chapter will discuss the importance of trust in repetitive coalition games: players often stay with a past coalition, despite present resource distribution, to maintain a stable alliance. Variable 4, not 7, predicts results. In American politics, those

---

[12] Jerome Chertkoff, "Sociopsychological Theories and Research on Coalition Formation," in *The Study of Coalition Behavior*, ed. Sven Groennings et al. (New York: Holt, Rinehart and Winston, 1970), p. 318; See also Chertkoff, "The Effects of Probability of Future Success on Coalition Formation," *Journal of Experimental Social Psychology* 2 (July 1966): 265–77.

[13] See W. Edgar Vinacke et al., "The Effect of Information about Strategy on a Three-Person Game," *Behavioral Science* 11 (May 1966): 180–89; and Bernhardt Lieberman, "i-Trust: A Notion of Trust in Three-Person Games and International Affairs," *Journal of Conflict Resolution* 21 (August 1956): 489–93.

members of Congress who are safe in their reelection develop years of experience with the game and with the other players. The same holds for bureaucrats and Supreme Court judges.

Overlapping membership (7) will also be discussed at length in a later chapter, but we can consider an example here. Suppose that triads ABC and BCD determine different outcomes in different political situations, but share the overlapping members of B and C. A BC coalition in one situation may constrain B's choice of D against C in a second situation, even though D has the advantage of initial resources.

Likeness or difference (5) between players and their *status ordering* (6) have similar critical effects. Status, as suggested earlier, may be socially or politically derived; likeness may be based on such things as age, sex, ideology, religion, the same cultural background. These variables affect communication among players and the choice of coalition partner. B and C may find it difficult to form a coalition, despite initial resources or other factors, if, quite literally, they cannot talk to each other—because they speak different languages or are not members of the same club.

Status order may be important in such diverse activities as revolutions or bureaucratic decisions. Robert Axelrod, for example, set forth what he called the *Clear the Cable* game for one game-theoretic application.[14] Two bureaucrats must agree in order to send a cable. If they disagree, they must refer the decision to their respective superiors and suffer a penalty for disturbing them. The superiors in turn can agree or delegate the decision to *their* superiors and also suffer a penalty by doing so. One factor critical to the game is the status differentiation among the players. Ideological distance has already been employed in a number of political studies, with the prediction that players closest to each other as measured on some ideological dimension will be most likely to form coalitions.[15] In short, effects of status and ideology, found throughout political activity, can be operationalized as factors affecting coalition formation.

The players' motivations in the game influence their bargaining strategies and results, independently of resources or other conditions. Most obviously, the players' *goals* (1) in the situation are critical. Many studies assume the goals as given, thus holding them constant. Nevertheless, some players seek the efficiency of a minimum win, some wish to control a coalition partner, and some desire the security of being part of the largest possible coalition. The work by Bueno de Mesquita and Niemi, cited in Chapter 3, used goals with initial resources to predict results.[16] Variable 1 with 8 predicts 18. In addition to specific goals, more general *attitudes toward winning and competition* (2) can affect behavior and results. These at-

[14] Robert Axelrod, *Conflict of Interest: A Theory of Divergent Goals with Applications to Politics* (Chicago: Markham, 1970), pp. 121–43.
[15] See, for example, the studies by DeSwaan and by Axelrod.
[16] Bruce Bueno de Mesquita and Richard Niemi, "A Dynamic Theory of Coalition Formation" (Paper delivered at Midwest Political Science Association Meeting Chicago, April 1980).

titudes can vary with cultural background, with personality, and with past socialization. Much of the research has focused on "exploitive" versus "accommodative" attitudes: the former seeking to maximize returns to the individual at the expense of others; the latter seeking a more even distribution of the winnings, or even an altruistic one.[17] One study related the need for achievement to various risk-taking strategies in three-person games.[18] Political oppression may be understood for its effects on people's goals and definitions of rationality and therefore on their coalition behavior.[19] Studies of political attitudes should be able to indicate other important distinctions.

The *stakes of the game* (12) affect motivation and results. Players, we expect, will bargain quite differently depending on whether exclusion from a winning coalition means retirement to the sea, renewed money-raising for the next campaign, or a beheading. Stakes include the magnitude as well as the range of gains or losses and the zero- or positive-sum character of the game. Stakes are represented in game theory by the payoff matrix; and recalling the examples from Chapter 2, we can see that the precise arrangement of payoffs in the matrix will affect the strategies that rational players will choose. Changing the payoff matrix changes the game and its solution. Thus, the precise arrangement of payoffs in the matrix can affect the nature of the coalition formed or whether one is formed. Stakes can be identified in experiments and described, even if impressionistically, in many real political situations. In game theory and experiments, the stakes are usually built into a game. They are held constant—treated as "given." However, in a few studies stakes have been deliberately varied. One study found that manipulating stakes affected the tendency to form stable coalitions.[20] Changes in stakes may also affect the tendency not to form a coalition.

Results will change depending on the *number of players* (11) and the *decision rules* (14) (e.g., a majority rule) that specify when a coalition may be said to occur. Rules permit or prohibit *positive or negative incentives* (16) to be added to influence bargaining. The "sidepayment," spoken of in game theory, is one such positive incentive. A sidepayment is a transfer of some payment, such as money, from one player to another either before or after a coalition has formed, and exists independently of the payoffs to the players. Group norms also pose incentives and influence people's bargaining: for example, a norm that one should hear all sides of a question and not reach hasty decisions, or a norm that encourages or frowns on sidepayments.

[17] M. V. Chaney and W. Edgar Vinacke, "Achievement and Nurturance in Triads Varying in Power Distribution," *Journal of Abnormal Social Psychology* 60 (1960): 175–81.

[18] Bruce Bueno de Mesquita, *Strategy, Risk and Personality in Coalition Politics: The Case of India* (Cambridge: Cambridge University Press, 1975).

[19] Virginia Sapiro, "Sex and Games: On Oppression and Rationality," *British Journal of Political Science* 9 (October 1979): 385–408.

[20] Bernhardt Lieberman, "Coalition Formation and Change," in *Social Choice*, ed. Bernhardt Lieberman (New York: Gordon and Breach Science, 1971), pp. 83–114. For another study showing the different effects of high and low stakes, see Morris Fiorina and Charles Plott, "Committee Decisions under Majority Rule: An Experimental Study," *American Political Science Review* 72 (June 1978): 575–98.

Rules dictate *when and under what conditions bargaining is permitted* (15) in experiments, mathematical formulations, or real-world cases. The rules can specify whether agreements reached during bargaining are enforceable or not, whether bargaining will be face-to-face or impersonal, and open or closed. In closed bargaining, a player makes an offer to another player, and the two bargain to see if they can form a coalition; in open bargaining, a player can make simultaneous offers to any number of other players. While the open bargaining condition appears most frequently in political situations, there are cases in which merely to initiate negotiations with one player inhibits or antagonizes other players and so precludes the chance of bargaining with them. Experiments have indicated that changes in this bargaining condition affect the choice of partner in winning coalitions.[21] Bargaining rules facilitate communication between some players more than others, as in seating arrangements, office location, or an official language necessary for parliamentary debate. Some experimental designs seat the players behind partitions, with placards to indicate choice of partner. This design screens out physical and personality effects (and in particular, variables 4–7), and produces different results from the face-to-face situation.[22] In the real world, technological development—air travel, road building, electronic communication—by increasing face-to-face bargaining and communication between players, can change the coalition formed.

The *information available* to players (17), as shaped by the rules and other political conditions, will also affect coalition formation. The clarity or confusion of information advantages some players over others.[23] Choice of partner changes as single information cues or multiple cues or no clear cues are provided (see Chapter 7). Rational players make different calculations in cases of full or imperfect information. Under conditions of uncertainty, players calculate the probabilities of success associated with the various strategies. Uncertainty, David Koehler argued, can lead to larger-than-minimum winning coalitions: given imperfect information about resources, players cannot afford to form minimum winning coalitions; instead, they will calculate the smallest possible coalition that will maximize their chance of winning.[24] In all of these cases, the effects change with a change in the information condition. Hence, simple rule changes—in physical location, telephone equipment, order of speaking, or limits on debate—can change the outcomes if some of the players who are otherwise disadvantaged can form

[21] See Jerome Chertkoff and Joseph Braden, "Effects of Experience and Bargaining Restrictions on Coalition Formation," *Journal of Personality and Social Psychology* 30 (July 1974): 169–77.

[22] Ibid.

[23] William Gamson, "Experimental Studies of Coalition Formation, " in *Advances in Experimental Social Psychology*, ed. Leonard Berkowitz (New York: Academic Press, 1964), pp. 81–110.

[24] David Koehler, "The Legislative Process and the Minimum Winning Coalition," in *Probability Models of Collective Decision Making*, ed. Richard Niemi and Herbert Weisberg (Columbus, Ohio: Charles Merrill, 1972), pp. 149–64, and "Legislative Coalition Formation," *American Journal of Political Science* 29 (February 1975): 27–39.

a coalition on the rules. Adding information, clarifying the situation, or deliberately confusing it will change the predicted political results.

Rules dictating the *recurrence of the game* (13) can change the stakes and experience with the game and with other players and so change the particular coalitions formed. Note the political implications of a terminal coalition situation: one directed to a final redistribution of power, ending the coalition situation and precluding its future occurrence. In a three-person game, two players join resources to dissolve the triad. They cash in their winnings and go home—or they eliminate the third player. Constitutional conventions and coup d'etats are obvious cases. Less obvious are cases of executive or legislative reorganization; decisions admitting or forbidding certain types of people to hold office; a law making certain political parties or campaign activities illegal. Equally interesting are the cases in which players know the situation will recur. These will be treated at length in the following chapter.

Consider the variety of political conditions indicated by the table. The variables can be easily operationalized and measured, yet they can be translated into historical patterns of consensus and cleavage, social status, cultural norms, turnover of members, frequency of occurrence, effects of multilingual customs, change in information technology, hierarchies as determined by formal constitutional arrangements, or institutional linkages such as federalism or separation of powers. They include such initial resources as votes, poll results, number of members in a legislature, energy resources, money, and war-making capacity. In other words, very complex political factors and interactions among such factors can be conceptualized and analyzed within such a scheme. We can inquire about the conditions under which formal properties of the game can be manipulated or controlled—how votes or weapons or election results are increased or reduced in importance. We can investigate within what limits—constitutionally, technologically, or historically derived—changes in these resources affect outcomes. Any of these influences can be analyzed or controlled. They explain who joins with whom, who wins and who loses, and who gets what; whether governing coalitions will persist over time; whether they upset, maintain, or reorganize the status order; whether decisions at one point in time or in one political arena will maintain or reverse decisions made elsewhere.

APPLICATION

The story is told of the astrophysicist and the microbiologist who were husband and wife—yet neither could quite believe in the existence of the other. The same sort of problem occurs with some of the variables as seen from the different research approaches. Many people will find the specific rules the least interesting part of the table. Holding the rules constant, they will prefer to focus on how the changes and interactions among the other variables affect coalition results. Other people, particularly game theorists, will find the rules the most interesting part of it, and manipulate them in order to identify various solutions. By defining such rules as whether sidepayments are permitted or whether agreements are enforceable, game theorists supply the necessary assumptions to achieve specific solutions for n-person games. All researchers will find some parts of the table more worthy of attention than other parts. Political scientists may be unhappy that key problems essential for analyzing their subjects have not been addressed in coalition research and so are not included in the table. Despite these dissatisfactions, the summary listing can have value. It can suggest additional assumptions to be introduced in n-person games[25] and additional controls to be imposed or manipulated in experiments. It can broaden the perspective of each approach and so focus attention on what may be of common interest to all.

Indeed, what is suggested by the list of variables is a sizable research schedule. Admittedly provisional and preliminary, it offers the *identification* of variables for analysis and control. This can sharpen our thinking about a subject, encourage more systematic analysis, and suggest new questions. It offers the *accumulation* of research results. Results for any one case, at one point in time, in one particular setting may contribute and be added to others. The schedule thus accommodates work in different approaches. Finally, it offers the *generalization* of such results. If we assume there are recurring patterns of coalition formation under various conditions, then these results ultimately can be applied and generalized to other situations. The advantage, then, of such a list of variables is threefold: it indicates for any one research area a schedule for further work, helps to accumulate that work, and relates it to work in other areas.

Take, for example, presidential nominations and, in particular, bandwagon effects. One study found that initial resources and ideological distance can predict the winning coalition formed.[26] The larger the initial number of delegate votes for a candidate, the more likely the candidate is to be included in a winning nominating coalition. Bandwagons, not minimum-winning coalitions, are formed. In terms of the present research schedule, variables 8 and 5 help predict 18. Other studies have tested the relative importance of variable 10 (probability of future election success) against variable 8.[27] We can now see other questions suggested by the table. How important is ideology in the nominating process? (i.e., how important is

[25] For a good discussion of the point, see Steven Brams, *Game Theory and Politics* (New York: Free Press, 1978), p. 200.

[26] James Zais and John Kessel, "A Theory of Presidential Nominations with a 1968 Illustration," in *Perspectives on Presidential Selection*, ed. Donald Matthews (Washington D.C.: Brookings, 1973), pp. 120–42.

[27] Chertkoff, "Probability of Success"; and William Gamson, "Coalition Formation at Presidential Nominating Conventions," *American Journal of Sociology* 68 (September 1962): 157–71.

variable 5 compared to the three initial-resource variables?) What are the effects of amateurs versus professionals (variable 4) in delegate composition? Are the results changed by changing information, as through news media reporting (variable 17), or by changes in convention or primary rules (variable 15)? How do these variables combine to affect the outcomes we wish to explain?

Even if one focuses only on conditions advantaging or disadvantaging frontrunners (22), a number of research questions are indicated from the table. They include

- At what point (9) and under what conditions does a candidate's initial advantage in resources become decisive?
- What is the relative importance of ideology (5) in modifying the effects of variable 9? What is the relative importance of either or both compared to the probability of future election success (10)?
- When and under what conditions can bandwagons be stopped? At what point (9) and under what other conditions (for example, 15 and 17) do such coalitions emerge? What are the parallels with other political situations also encouraging temporary alliances and discouraging durable ones?
- How, specifically, do bargaining and information conditions (15 and 17) advantage the initially strongest player?[28] Recent reforms have limited the demonstrations and other confusion in the convention hall. There are improved communication systems between candidates and state delegations. Other changes have increased the amount of information available at the primary stage. We can ask whether and how these changes have affected coalition behavior and results.

Such studies can contribute to an understanding of coalition-formation processes beyond the nominating event. Bandwagons are popularly associated with presidential nominations, but they are not limited to these. In many political situations, an appearance of strength may be decisive. So we can ask, more generally, about the conditions facilitating or inhibiting bandwagon effects, in combination with or controlling for other variables on the list. Presidential nominating studies would become a contributing case, and the broader study in turn would help to place presidential bandwagons in clearer perspective.

The same kind of exercise could be carried out for any political subject. One can take the forming of a government in a multi-party system, the passage of a bill in Congress, or the problems of alliances between nations, and try a similar working through of possible questions. Since the various subject matters may themselves be combined—within the framework suggested by the table—one can begin to see just how sizable a research schedule is proposed.

[28] Barbara Hinckley, "The Initially Strongest Player: Coalition Games and Presidential Nominations," *American Behavioral Scientist* 18 (March/April 1975): 497–512.

Chapter 5

Coalitions in Time

It is the Spring Campaign of 1903. France moves an army into the Ruhr and a fleet from Marseilles to Piedmont. England, leaving London and the English Channel unprotected, has fleets in the North Sea, and at Norway and Portugal. The French army in Gascony, rather than moving to face a threat from the East, supports an English attack on Spain. As every player of the game *Diplomacy*[1] knows, this is very typical behavior. The Anglo-French coalition has found that both achieve more by playing together than by playing alone. They can trust each other and gain the luxury of leaving their mutual coasts unprotected. They sacrifice immediate short-term gains for the gains of the alliance over time. The outcomes are determined—and the map of Europe redivided—by the players' perceptions that the game continues over time.

The single game, however, has been heavily emphasized in coalition research. This holds both for the mathematical games and the social-psychological experiments. Players come together in a game that has no past or future. They do not know each other and assume they will not meet thereafter. They come together "out of time" to play once for one outcome.

Some existing studies, it is true, have worked with a time dimension. Games in game theory can be divided into those of finite and indeterminate length, and some indeterminate-length games have been analyzed fully.[2] At-

---

[1] Games Research, Boston, 1961.

[2] Martin Shubik, "Game Theory and the Study of Social Behavior," in *Game Theory and Related Approaches to Social Behavior*, ed. Martin Shubik (New York: John Wiley, 1964), pp. 61–70.

tempts are being made to deal mathematically with sequential and probabilistic steps in bargaining and choice of partner,[3] and models have been developed analyzing games played with accumulated scoring.[4] The dynamics of bandwagon formation has been studied, as we saw in the example in Chapter 2. Social psychologists have examined the tendency to unite against the leader,[5] the feedback from bargaining over a series of games,[6] and the effects of trust and deception.[7] These cases, however, remain the exception.

The single game, of course, is the simplest and most feasible of designs. A game of Parcheesi, played once, tests coalition behavior under controlled conditions. Played twenty times, it might only test human response to boring situations. By eliminating a social context, researchers concentrate on the pure relationships of the play. Yet in sharp contrast, real political games occur in time. They occur as one of an experienced or expected series, where players know each other and expect to meet and play again.

Even in a single game, players share a past and some expectations about the returns being awarded. Bargaining is shaped by historical alliances. Deception is constrained by the risk of retaliation. The victorious revolutionaries will have to run a government. The single-game situation, then, deliberately excludes the temporal context within which political activity occurs.

Consider, for example, some cases in which minimum winning coalitions do not form. For one case, social norms concerning competition and bargaining may lead players to form a more inclusive coalition than mini-

[3] See, for example, J. Harsnyi, "A Solution Theory for Non-cooperative Games: Its Implications for Cooperative Games," in *Game Theory and Political Science*, ed. Peter Ordeshook (New York: New York University Press, 1978), pp. 39–95; and James Kahan and Amnon Rapoport, "Test of the Bargaining Set and Kernel Models in Three Person Games," in *Game Theory as a Theory of Conflict Resolution*, ed. Anatol Rapoport (Boston: D. Reidel, 1974), pp. 119–60.

[4] See James Laing and Richard Morrison, "Coalitions and Payoffs in Three-Person Games: Initial Tests of Two Formal Models," *Journal of Mathematical Sociology* 3 (1973): 3–25, and "Coalitions and Payoffs in Three-Person Supergames under Multiple-Trial Agreements," in *Game Theory as a Theory of Conflict Resolution*, pp. 207–34; Bruce Bueno de Mesquita, *Strategy, Risk and Personality in Coalition Politics: The Case of India* (Cambridge: Cambridge University Press, 1975); Bruce Bueno de Mesquita and Richard Niemi, "A Dynamic Theory of Coalition Formation," (Paper delivered at Midwest Political Science Association Meeting, Chicago, April 1980).

[5] See P. Hoffman et al., "Tendencies Toward Group Comparability in Competitive Bargaining," *Human Relations* 7 (May 1954): 141–59; and H. A. Michener and E. J. Lawler, "Revolutionary Coalition Strength and Collective Failure as Determinants of Status Reallocation," *Journal of Experimental Social Psychology* 7 (July 1971): pp. 448–60.

[6] S. S. Komorita and Jerome Chertkoff, "A Bargaining Theory of Coalition Formation," *Psychology Review* 80 (May 1973): 149–62; Jerome Chertkoff, "Sociopsychological Views on Sequential Effects in Coalition Formation," *American Behavioral Scientist* 18 (March/April 1975): 451–71.

[7] For summary, see Bernhardt Lieberman, "Coalitions and Conflict Resolution," *American Behavioral Scientist* 18 (March/April 1975): 557–81.

mum size.[8] For a second, players form larger-than-minimum coalitions to increase the probability of future success.[9] For a third, players choose a past coalition partner to obtain a larger-than-minimum victory, reasoning that over the long haul a stable, "trusted" coalition will bring the greatest return.[10] And for a fourth, minimum winning coalitions may be prohibited from forming because of the ideological distance or historical animosity existing between potential coalition partners.[11]

Summaries of this research conclude that there are a number of important factors other than initial resource distribution that may affect outcomes.[12] There may, however, be a simpler and more comprehensive interpretation possible. Each of these cases assumes a time span *longer than a single game*. From this shift in time perspective come alternate cues: other information to help the players choose a coalition partner. We find the importance of trust or future success or past hostility, the importance of norms developed over time or invoked to keep the group together—to play again another day. In other words, the initial resource variable and the minimum winning solution derived from it may be peculiarly important to the single game. In a time-contingent situation, knowing the initial resource distribution is not sufficient to predict the outcome.

So imagine a situation in which A leads B who in turn leads C in initial resources. We would expect B and C to form a minimum winning coalition against A—unless any of the following information were available:

> B is supposed to be an untrustworthy ally.
> An ACD coalition situation is likely to occur next week.
> A and C are male; B is female.
> A and C formed a coalition last year in a similar situation.

When there is a future to consider, the size of the winning in one game may affect the bargaining position later. People usually prefer to bargain

[8] Barry Collins and Bertram Raven, "Group Structure: Attraction, Coalitions, Communication and Power," in the *Handbook of Social Psychology*, 2nd ed., ed. Gardner Lindzey and Elliot Aronson (Reading, Mass.: Addison-Wesley, 1969), 4: 127–37. See also Donald Lutz and James Williams, *Minimum Coalitions in Legislatures: A Review of the Evidence*, Sage Professional Paper #04–028 (Beverly Hills and London: Sage Publications, January 1976).

[9] Jerome Chertkoff, "The Effects of Probability of Future Success on Coalition Formation," *Journal of Experimental Social Psychology* 2 (1966): 265–77.

[10] Bernhardt Lieberman, "Experimental Studies of Conflict in Some Two-Person and Three-Person Games," in *Mathematical Methods in Small Group Processes*, ed. J. Criswell et al. (Stanford University Press, 1962), pp. 203–20, and "i-Trust: A Notion of Trust in Three-Person Games and International Affairs," *Journal of Conflict Resolution* 8 (1964): 271–80. See also Barbara Hinckley, "Coalitions in Congress: Size in a Series of Games," *American Politics Quarterly* 1 (July 1973): 339–59.

[11] See essays by Michael Leiserson and by Abram DeSwaan in *The Study of Coalition Behavior*, ed. Sven Groennings et al. (New York: Holt, Rinehart and Winston, 1970).

[12] See, for example, the excellent review in Jerome Chertkoff, "Sociopsychological Theories and Research in Coalition Formation," in *Study of Coalition Behavior*, p. 315; and Collins and Raven, "Group Structures," pp. 136, 137.

from a position of strength rather than weakness. In such situations, initially strongest A is no longer necessarily excluded and may indeed be sought by both of the other players. Resources are spent as investment in future games, and coalition AB or AC may be expected to form—outcomes different from the BC coalition predicted for the single game. When there is a past, players know what has worked before—though under different initial-resource conditions. Different coalitions will be predicted depending on those past returns. With both a past and a future, players may reason that a stable coalition will bring the greatest return and prefer to stay with a past partner, despite present resource distribution, to maximize returns over all games. Thus in any one game in a series, the past choice of partner may be the best predictor of present coalition formation.

For another illustration, recall the four "theories" from the social-psychological studies set forth in Chapter 2: minimum-resource theory, minimum-power theory, anticompetitive theory, and random choice. Underlying these categories, we suggested, were different kinds of information made important for the players; that is, different salient cues for decision. That idea can now be taken one step further. William Gamson indicated, perhaps with tongue-in-cheek, the ideal "demonstrations" (not tests) that would support each of the four theories.[13] He made no systematic attempt to isolate these factors, but two that he uses throughout should be discussed. These concern *experience with the game* and *experience with the other players*. Both require a location of the game in time.

Experience with the game is different for three of the four demonstrations. For minimum-power theory Gamson suggested that we give the subjects "ample opportunity for learning in a situation which is simple enough for them eventually to perceive the pivotal power of the players." This is not provided for in minimum-resource theory, although the game is kept simple enough to perceive the importance of initial resources. For a random-choice demonstration, even that simplicity is removed. A situation of general confusion, complexity, and difficult rules will not permit learning or any clear perception of initial resource importance.

Experience with the players is also highlighted for three of the four situations. For minimum-power, Gamson advised, "use subjects who have no established social relation with each other and no prospects of a continuing relation after the experiment." For random-choice, he said "make sure that subjects do not know each other previously and are unlikely to encounter each other in the future." But for anticompetitive theory, he suggested, "subjects should be used who already have a friendly relation with each other and who will continue their association after the experiment is over."

We find, then, that the various situations change the perceived importance of initial resources relative to other cues. Learning by the players permits alternative perceptions in the minimum-power case. Experience with

---

[13] William Gamson, "Experimental Studies of Coalition Formation," in *Advances in Experimental Social Psychology*, ed. L. Berkowitz (New York: Academic Press, 1964), pp. 103–06.

the players permits alternative perceptions in the anticompetitive case. Neither experience with the players nor opportunity for learning permits alternative perceptions in the random-choice case; nor is the situation clear enough to perceive even the initial resource cues. The minimum-resource case permits perceptions of initial resources but excludes the learning and experience with players for any alternative perceptions. It highlights only initial resources.

Together, the cases suggest that the importance of the initial resource variable is found primarily in the single-game situation in which no other information is provided. There, B joins with C because there is really no good reason to do otherwise. There are no alternate cues. In other situations, past events and future expectations expand and complicate the choice. Initial resources, then, are reduced in importance by the location of any one event in time.

This chapter proposes that coalition activity need not be interpreted as a static concept applied to dynamic political events. Indeed, distinguishing such activity by its occurrence in time will increase applicability, improve explanatory power, and begin to isolate key patterns of behavior from each other. The chapter will elaborate this distinction, outline the effects of time on coalition behavior, and then examine one case of these effects: the importance of trust in politics.

COALITIONS IN AND OUT OF TIME: A CLASSIFICATION

The single game stipulates one gathering of players in one situation with one distribution of returns. Time provides the possibility of plural occurrences on all three dimensions. We thus find four distinct kinds of coalition situations, which are summarized in Table 5.1.

Beyond the single game, emphasized in past studies, three other situations can be distinguished. In *time-contingent single games*, players play once for one outcome. There is a single event, but the players—or at least some significant portion of them—have met before or expect to meet again. In *cumulative games*, players play more than once for a single final outcome. There is only one outcome to be determined, but there is a repetition of coalition activity leading to that outcome. In *repetitive games*, players play several games for several outcomes. Players gather, engage in coalition activity, and determine outcomes over time. Any single event is part of a series of like events.[14]

[14] Cf. Theodore Caplow's classification of "continuous," "episodic," and "terminal situations" in "Further Development of a Theory of Coalitions in the Triad," *American Journal of Sociology* 64 (March 1959): 489. His terms suggest the importance of time, with each word referring to a way of cutting into or not cutting into a time dimension. But the distinction—

Table 5.1   Four Kinds of Coalition Activity

| | NUMBER OF TIMES | | |
TYPE OF GAME	The Players Gather	A Game Is Played	An Outcome Is Determined
Single games	once	once	once
Time-contingent single games	more than once	once	once
Cumulative games	more than once	more than once	once
Repetitive games	more than once	more than once	more than once

We can classify a wide range of political situations, distinguishing them by the kinds of information provided and the kinds of variables important in explaining results. (The list of variables from the preceding chapter can be used as a checklist for the discussion.)

In *time-contingent single games* players know more about other players than their initial resources. Characteristics other than their game-playing behavior become important: for example, likeness to each other, status, past hostilities or friendships, overlapping membership (e.g., an international summit, a single-ballot nominating convention, a palace revolution). In contrast to single games, we would thus expect variables 5–7 in Table 4.1 to override the predictions of the initial resource variables 8 and 9. Moreover, we would expect these effects to hold in diverse situations similar only in being time-contingent single games.

In *cumulative games* players gain experience with the game and with the other players. Learned behavior through the sequence becomes important (e.g., a multi-ballot nominating convention, multi-stage budget decisions, candidate blocs in a series of presidential primaries for one final distribution of delegate votes). We would thus expect variables 3 and 4 to help predict outcomes independently of initial resources and of variables 5–7. Learning overrides such other information as initial resources, status barriers, or social stereotyping, with the result that the past is discounted against the present performance. Hence, we would expect skill and behavior in the game to override past reputation and resources in a range of situations similar only in the cumulative nature of the play.

---

and the importance of Caplow's classification—actually rests on the different *objectives* of the game and not on a distinction among temporal situations. These objectives are not necessarily related to the situating of events in time; at least, Caplow offers no elaboration of any such relationship.

In *repetitive games* players have all of the above information plus the results of past games and the expectation that the game will recur (e.g., legislative roll calls, unsettled boundary disputes, continuous economic conferences). Variables 3 and 4 remain important, but the past results (especially 18 and 23) now become part of the information predicting future outcomes. At the extreme, we might predict that the most likely coalition to form is the coalition that formed before.

The classification suggests that major predictive variables can be identified and subsequent hypotheses derived only after knowing the situation of the game in time. It follows that any modification in the timing of a game may change the benefits and disadvantages of various players. Increase the repetition, discourage past friendships, divide bargaining into a series of stages—and one changes the coalition predicted. In addition, the classification warns that superficially like or unlike processes need to be distinguished by their location in time. Compare legislative assemblies making frequent, repetitive decisions with those meeting briefly, intermittently, and with little continuity among the members. Superficially unlike events, too, as in the examples suggested above, should show similar coalition behavior transcending national or institutional form.

COALITION BEHAVIOR IN REPETITIVE GAMES

The repetitive case is worth tracing at length for its frequency and importance in political settings. Assume coalition actors seek to maximize their share of success from the situation with the least cost to their own resources: in single games, from the one distribution of rewards; in repetitive games, from the summed distribution over all games. Each game is played for itself, for its own returns; the overall goal is to maximize total returns. The costs, like the returns, can be more or less material. Communication costs, the amount of effort required, and the psychic strain of uncertainty and risk are all part of the calculation.[15] The only difference lies in the repetition of the play; however, behavior in any one game in a series will differ sharply from the single-game result.

In repetitive games, players have the results of past games plus the recognition that the game will recur. They may reason that over the long haul a stable coalition will bring the greatest return. Uncertainty is reduced, communication is made easier as a result of past learning, players' bargaining styles are known. We expect that maintaining a coalition would be easier than forming a new one, the effort made less by the effort expended before. All these factors may lead to a choice of past partner, despite the

---

[15] Charles Adrian and Charles Press, "Decision Costs in Coalition Formation," *American Political Science Review* 62 (June 1968): 556–63.

present resource distribution: in short, the best predictor of coalition formation is the coalition which formed before. The more a situation is repeated, the more advantage comes to such a coalition: there is less uncertainty to face, effort to spend, risk to take. We may find, then, in situations repeating over time, that stable coalitions will form.

Another effect is suggested by the process of repetition. In any single game, rules and resources are externally imposed—by events in the world outside or by the artifice imposed by the experimenter. The votes or the weapons or the red and blue markers have been allocated; the rules are predetermined. While repetitive games are subject to the same external imposition, other rules and resources develop over the course of play. Group norms and other learning impose new rules. Past victories and defeats shape new resources. The result may be considerable independence from external effects as those produced "internally"—by or as a by-product of the coalition situation itself—become more important.

Every two years following an election, the American Congress selects the members who will chair its powerful standing committees. The decision requires coalition formation; since it occurs every two years, it is a repetitive coalition case. Under the rules, new coalitions might form with each new congress, depending on the change in number and resources of the elected members. Northeastern liberals might bargain for some committee chairs, assuring Western representatives the leadership, say, of all energy-related committees. Conservative members could counterbargain, offering the Westerners energy and a share of defense. The committee chairs would then be alloted in part by the strength of the various congressional factions, as determined by the election. The initial distribution of resources would be important. However, this process does not occur. Instead, a "seniority norm" has developed in the Congress, giving the committee chairs to those members with longest consecutive service on the committee. A faction, dwindling in numbers but strong in seniority, gains chairs in this particular coalition situation that it would not gain in others. In this repetitive coalition case, a new rule—one about seniority—has developed over the course of play.

TRUST

One other effect of repetition is important enough to be considered in more detail. It concerns the importance of trust in maintaining alliances and the behavior devoted to developing and keeping it.

Bernhardt Lieberman advanced the notion of *i*-trust, in which the *i* stands for *interest*—or more precisely self-interest. Trust is important in repetitive games, said Lieberman, not because it is morally or ethically good, but because it maximizes success over a number of games even at the cost of sacrificing immediate gain.[16]

In Lieberman's experiment, twenty-four undergraduates formed eight separate groups of three players. Each group of three players (that is, each triad) played forty repetitions of the same game. Five of the groups developed considerable coalition stability over the forty trials, changing coalitions less than ten times. Three of these five groups changed coalitions only twice over the forty games. The remaining three groups did not develop stable coalitions. Whether they would do so after learning the overall results of the forty trials could not be answered from this particular experimental situation. Some players may have "learned the game" faster than others.

According to Lieberman, the five groups that developed stable coalitions recognized that trust was important. In one group player A and player C had been in coalition in previous trials. When player C was being tempted by a particularly attractive offer from B, C responded, "I *must* trust [A] and he can trust me. If I leave him, you'll wonder if I might leave you. Then if you two team up, I'll have nowhere to turn." The importance of trust was voiced repeatedly in the bargaining: in one group one player said, "I have found that I cannot take [A] at his word. Disappointed as I am, I would be willing to listen to any offer you make"; in another, "If you trust me, I will offer you an [even] split." In one other group, A was attempting to break the BC alliance by pointing out to C that B had broken an alliance before. C responded, "If I broke my alliance with [B], I'd be no better than him. I owe him one hand. Next time around I'll consider it." C was trying to maintain the past alliance with B, while at the same time keeping his options open and developing trust with A. Players in these groups, then, tended to fulfill their commitments even at the sacrifice of immediate gain.

The relevance to many real political games is clear. In the House of Representatives, as Richard Fenno remarked, "exchanges of trust . . . pervade every attempt to exercise influence in the chamber."[17] Against the advances of the conservative coalition, House Democratic Whip Hale Boggs warned southern colleagues that Republicans were "untrustworthy allies"—

---

[16] Lieberman, "*i*-Trust." The experiment was based on a three-person, zero-sum majority game with the following payoff structure:

　　If coalition AB formed, the coalition received 10¢ from C.
　　If coalition AC formed, the coalition received 8¢ from B.
　　If coalition BC formed, the coalition received 6¢ from A.

At the beginning of the game, each player was given $3.00. The game involved two steps: first, bargaining by written communication as to how winnings would be divided if the players were indeed to form a coalition, and second, the decision following the bargaining. The decision was made by players placing a card designating their choice of partner face down on the table. So at the moment of decision each player did not know the choices of the others. Three distinct coalitions were possible. On any one play, only one coalition or none at all could occur.

[17] "The Initial Distribution of Influence: The House," in *The Congress and America's Future*, 2nd ed., ed. David Truman (Englewood Cliffs, N.J.: Prentice-Hall, 1965), p. 189.

as he had learned early in his House career.[18] Lieberman applied the concept to international relations:

> It is often in the interest of a nation or group of nations to keep an agreement, not for immediate gain—even contrary to this consideration—but in the interest of its coalition structure. A nation may take an action contrary to its immediate self-interest, or when its own self-interest is unclear, in order to promote the stability of its coalition structure. It has long been obvious to statesmen and it was demonstrated in the particular laboratory experiment reported here that rewards and payoffs often come to the stable alliance, and that an alliance has stability when its members can be reasonably certain that their partners will not desert them for some temporary gain.[19]

The importance of trust is based on the recognition that the game will be repeated over time—in the forty trials of the experiment, legislative roll calls, or international affairs.

Other Forms of Trust

The players in Lieberman's game relied on behavior repeated over time. Trust, however, also springs from past experiences outside the game: from experiences with the other players either as individuals or as representatives of a class. Player A trusts B on the city council because they have worked on real estate matters before or because B, though a stranger, represents a group with a predictable land-development policy. Third-world nations may turn first to each other as coalition partners before approaching their former colonizers.

Trust becomes critical in a real-world context—where events occur in time, pose uncertainties, require economies of decision. Such a context permits the development of trust and supplies its importance. A player, faced with uncertainty and many other things to do, seeks a trustworthy partner as the quickest, easiest, surest way to maximize a share of returns. Likeness, historical memory, repetition of the game—all suggest who is to be trusted. The reliance on the past in repetitive situations is, then, merely one kind of trust that may displace or substitute for others.

Changing the game merely by adding or removing repetition can change results by substituting one kind of trust for another. Thus repetition could reduce the effects of social prejudice in a political decision-making body. One trusts people who are similar to oneself in class or status or social

---

[18] John Manley, "The Conservative Coalition in Congress," *American Behavioral Scientist* 17 (November/December 1973): 234.

[19] Lieberman, "*i*-Trust," p. 272.

background, *or* one trusts people one has developed confidence in through repeated decisions. The latter kind of trust can replace the former in influence.

Keeping the Trust

Given the importance of maintaining stable alliances, players may sacrifice much to "keep the trust" between partners. One discussion of this is found in Caplow's analysis of linked triads in the family. Caplow proposed that, "In a set of linked triads, a coalition partner in one triad may not be an opponent in another." He elaborated:

> When an actor is invited to join two potential coalitions, so situated that his partner, if he joined one coalition, would be his opponent if he joined the other coalition, the coalitions in question are *incompatible*. He must choose one (or neither), but he cannot choose both. . . . (Caplow's italics)[20]

Caplow suggested that one way such incompatible coalitions can be managed is with avoidance relationships, such as those instituted between married partners and mothers-in-law. The point of mother-in-law avoidance is that it prevents the married partners from having to choose between two incompatible coalitions: one valuable in the family of origin, the other in the family he or she has entered. Both coalitions can be maintained as long as they are kept, by social norm or individual choice, strictly separate. In situations where such avoidance is not maintained (for example, when one mother-in-law lives with the couple), at least one of the two valuable coalitions will dissolve. C cannot treat B both as a partner and as an opponent.[21]

The joking relationship between more remote relatives is another case in point. Joking permits nonpartners to remain friendly with each other while signaling publicly that they have not formed a coalition.[22] Here, a choice can be made between two incompatible coalitions. One is assumed to be more valuable than the other—valuable in the sense of producing greater returns. In the mother-in-law situation, no such choice is possible. Each is assumed to be equally valuable. Both cases, however, assert that, assuming decisions over time, one player cannot be both in coalition and in opposition with another.

The point is worth some political study. To what extent can "trust-threatening" behavior between coalition partners be tolerated and across

---

[20] Theodore Caplow, *Two Against One: Coalitions in Triads* (Englewood Cliffs, New Jersey: Prentice-Hall, 1968), p. 59.
[21] Ibid., pp. 103–8.
[22] Ibid., p. 108.

what range of situations? What kind of exceptions are permitted and what activities would result? Can symbolic actions be identified whereby both partners and nonpartners assure all the parties involved that the coalition is indeed being maintained despite appearances to the contrary? If so, such symbolic action is important communication in any continuing coalition situation.[23]

Conflict between partners can be considered an extreme threat to trust. Thus stable alliances can determine the range and kind of conflict possible *for all actors*: in effect, prohibiting conflict in one sphere that would threaten the trust between traditional partners in another sphere. Take, for example, the situation in which the same actors face over time a range of very diverse issues. Stable partners on one set of issues may prefer to remain inactive on another set of issues rather than threaten the trust by opposing each other. They remain inactive—and sacrifice any immediate returns—to maximize returns over time. Alternatively, stable partners on one set of issues may join in coalition to suppress a potentially disruptive issue from even arising. It appears to be a nonevent, since it never gets to the agenda, though in fact a coalition situation has occurred. Both possibilities would lead to the following results: (1) stable partners on one set of issues would not be found in opposition on other issues, and (2) given any change in the traditional alignment, there would be a corresponding change in the kinds of issues producing conflict. The "trouble spots" in one area would appear or disappear because of coalitions formed in another area.

In all these questions, one asks what behavior may be associated with "keeping the trust" in repetitive situations. Trust in politics may be so pervasive as to be taken for granted, its very pervasiveness obscuring the number of activities devoted to maintaining it, developing it in the first place, or finding substitutes in its absence.

COMBINED REPETITIVE AND CUMULATIVE GAMES

In a fully repetitive situation, each game is played for itself, for its own returns. In some games, however, the rules permit *convertible payoffs*: that is, the winnings or losings in one game convert to gains or losses in the next. They become part of the base resources for future games. *Diplomacy* players lose or gain fleets and armies, as a result of one game, and these form the

---

[23] See Thomas Franck and Edward Weisband, *Word Politics: Verbal Strategy Among the Superpowers* (New York: Oxford University Press, 1972). Franck and Weisband describe dyadic (two-nation) relationships, but their discussion could easily be extended to coalition bargaining. See esp. pp. 113–36; 148–69.

new resource base for the next. What this rule means, in effect, is that players are playing *two* games simultaneously: the repetitive game we have considered previously and a longer-range cumulative game for some future or indefinite final accounting.

We should expect that outcomes under this variation in the rules would differ from the strictly repetitive game. Since the games are played repetitively, the stability of alliances and trust between partners should remain important. But since the games are also played cumulatively, other factors may limit both stability and trust. On occasion, treachery, not trust, may offer greater rewards. With a stable AC alliance and convertible payoffs, C may eventually surpass the initially stronger B in resources and begin to consider the advantages of a CB coalition.[24] Cumulative games show some evidence of coalitions forming against the strongest player. Bargaining strategies—in which players ask for what appears to be too much or too little—can change results.[25]

We can also note the possibility of one player achieving dictatorial power in the situation: the repeatedly successful player may gain so much that he or she does not need to form coalitions, but can determine outcomes alone. The frequent occurrence of dictatorial power in real political cases attests to the viability of this outcome, but leads to a number of follow-up questions. Are other players acting rationally by gaining short-run returns from an advantageous coalition but suffering ultimate domination by a dictatorial player? At what point and under what conditions might dictatorial outcomes best be prohibited by forming opposing coalitions? Are there occasions when even the potentially dictatorial player might rationally decide not to end the coalition situation? Token "losses" to an opposing coalition or unnecessary generosity to a partner might preserve the present very rewarding series of games.

Repetitive games with convertible payoffs have been modelled formally[26] and played experimentally,[27] although they have not been distinguished from other repetitive or cumulative games. There are few enough writers concerned with the dynamics of coalition formation; it is not surprising that the distinctions among the games have yet to be articulated. The classification proposed in this chapter may ultimately not prove useful. It can, however, serve as a first step toward distinguishing the kind of dynamic games occurring, the different predictions about outcomes, and their political implications.

---

[24] See Bueno de Mesquita and Niemi, "Coalition Formation."

[25] Chertkoff, "Sociopsychological Views on Sequential Effects in Coalition Formation."

[26] See Bueno de Mesquita and Niemi, "Coalition Formation"; Bueno de Mesquita, *Strategy, Risk, and Personality*; Laing and Morrison, "Coalitions and Payoffs in Three-Person Games," and "Coalitions and Payoffs in Three-Person Supergames."

[27] See the studies by Laing and Morrison and see Chertkoff, "Sociopsychological Views on Sequential Effects in Coalition Formation."

This chapter extended the application of coalitions beyond the single game, proposed a classification for games played in and out of time, and elaborated some predictions for the different situations. The repetitive game was treated at length because of its importance and frequency of occurrence in politics. Merely repeating a coalition situation over time, with some frequency, regularity, and familiarity among the actors may lead to a number of specific activities of political consequence: (1) the reduced importance of initial resources, (2) choice of past partner for a stable alliance, (3) independence from external influences as new rules and resources are developed through experience in the situation, and (4) activities associated with keeping the trust. Nations, legislators, bureaucrats, captains of industry, and military elites all face coalition situations repeatedly. With information about past results and recognition that the game will recur, coalition behavior tends to stabilize, crystallize, and take on a life of its own.

Therefore, those concerned with increasing the importance of initial resources, changing the status quo, or introducing new issues previously suppressed, would be directed to changing the repetitive nature of the game. They should try to increase turnover (column one in Table 5.1), or decrease the frequency of interaction (column two), or limit the occasions when decisions are made (column three). They can discourage informal contacts, limit the number of meetings, shuffle the players representing England and France, postpone the Fall Campaign to some indefinite date.

These arguments have been advanced to illustrate the possible effects of time on coalition behavior. They should help to identify similar behavior in diverse settings and to clarify what is occurring in any one setting. They can be treated as hypotheses and subjected to testing. They can be elaborated more fully. Repetition, for example, has been treated here as a summary, discrete category; yet the degree of repetition may have important effects as well. Other hypotheses could be developed for repetitive games and for the cumulative and time-contingent situations. Distinctions need to be made for games with and without convertible payoffs. Stable coalitions, presumably, would not be expected to form in all repetitive situations under all conditions. The size of the stakes or a change in the bargaining conditions could change results. There are other occasions, as we will see in the following chapter, in which unpredictability and instability have advantages. Players wish to make known that they may or may not be available to form a coalition, and that whatever they do this time will not necessarily affect next time. To raise the arguments is not to say that they would hold alone or hold in all cases, but to suggest that where and when they hold is worth investigation.

As a beginning, take the political convention game (Chapter 2), Lieberman's experiment, or any problem in which three individuals must choose their preferred coalition partner. Play the game once and report results. Immediately repeat the same game and again report results. Then announce to the players that the same game will be repeated twice more and report these results. Have the results changed merely by changing the repetition? This simple experiment could be expanded to include other effects, such as those identified in Chapter 4. Players could be selected for their likeness or unlikeness to each other, by sex or age, by their past friendships or by sitting beside each other. The stakes could be changed or the initial resources varied. The rule about convertible payoffs can be changed. How important, then, is repetition, compared to any of these other factors? And under what conditions will repetition be important in determining results?

Work on the dynamics of coalition formation is still in its early stages, but the political implications should be clear. In the course of this short analysis, we have discussed maintaining the status quo, subverting dictatorships, building trust in stable alliances, strategies to override social prejudice, and the uses of symbolic communication in coalition bargaining. These and other political problems can be classified and addressed by studying the occurrence of coalitions in time.

Chapter 6

Coalitions in Political Space

Political actors work within a larger political environment: they affect and are affected by actions beyond their immediate spheres. Coalition analysis provides ways of studying these larger environmental linkages. Just as coalitions are rarely isolated in time, they are also rarely isolated in political "space": coalition behavior in one situation both affects and is affected by behavior in other situations.

Two major ways of analyzing these linkages have already been discussed. In Chapter 4, environmental effects were viewed as independent variables affecting coalition behavior and results. A larger social environment shapes the likeness among actors, their past experiences with each other, their status, and their attitudes toward competition and what constitutes fair play. Rules and bargaining conditions can be defined by factors external to the game. Initial resources are determined. Indeed, the scheme set out in Table 4.1 suggests a way of synthesizing a large and complex range of environmental influences on coalition results. The results, in turn, imply further environmental impact—in the stability or revolution or particular governing coalition they produce. In Chapter 5, time provided the linkage with environment. Socialization and other past experiences provide information and substitutes for trust. Rules and resources for any one situation were set elsewhere and previously; coalitions formed in that situation set other rules and resources in turn. Many of the feedback processes diagramed in political system flow charts can be thought of as just such a process of rule- and resource-setting in one situation for another, over time.

A third way of analyzing these linkages will be addressed in this chapter. It is a structural analysis, based on the notion of overlapping membership in coalition situations and derived from Theodore Caplow's work with linked triads. Politics is not neatly circumscribed or arranged around separate game boards. Coalition actors in one situation are affected by their calculations in another situation. They are linked to other actors by the political roles they are expected to pursue. Hence, we need to investigate the interdependence among coalition situations and seek ways to analyze these different linkage effects.

Caplow's work is offered here mainly as extended example of the kind of structural analysis possible. Caplow worked with triads, measured power by formal status rankings, and assumed a finite (limited) universe of these linked triads. Any of these assumptions can be questioned, and these questions and others will become clearer as the chapter proceeds. As illustration, however, the example suggests additional ways by which coalition analysis can address complex, interdependent political actions. This chapter, then, will extend the discussion into the "space" of the larger political environment, offer an illustration of such an extension, and pay closer attention to some of the variables introduced in Chapter 4.

CAPLOW'S LINKED TRIADS

In Caplow's analysis, coalitions are linked by overlapping membership.[1] Triads are linked when they have one or two members in common: triads ABC and BCD are linked by the overlapping membership of B and C. B and C therefore bring to either coalition situation the information and experience supplied from the other situation. In addition to overlapping membership, Caplow used initial resource distribution. He gave the variable an ordinal measurement, based on formal status rankings, and called it the "power distribution" among the actors. All actors can be ranked by their power in relationship to others, and the triads themselves can be ranked by the power of their members. In comparing linked triads ABC and BCD, in which the actors are designated alphabetically by the amount of power from strongest A to weakest D, Caplow called ABC the superior triad. Figure 6.1 is a representation of this kind of power ranking. It shows how such linkages can affect coalition formation in any one triad and how they can reorganize relationships between triads.

Caplow employed two predictive principles: (1) In a set of linked triads, a coalition partner in one triad may not be an opponent in another; (2) In a set of linked triads, an actor who is offered a choice between incompatible winning coalitions ("incompatible" from point 1) will choose the winning coalition in the superior triad.[2]

---

[1] *Two Against One: Coalitions in Triads* (Englewood Cliffs, N.J.: Prentice-Hall, 1968), p. 167.
[2] Ibid., p. 59.

Using only these two principles, he was able to predict which coalition would form in each of the linked triads, the extent to which there would be a range of choice, and what the particular problem areas might be. Coalition formation in any one triad is affected by its relations to other triads and in turn reshapes relations in the entire chain of linked triads. If the chain of linked triads is considered a political environment for any one set of actors in a situation, that environment can directly affect and be affected by a particular case of coalition formation.

We can apply this scheme, with Caplow's illustrations, to three linkage relationships of particular political interest: vertical hierarchies; horizontal "peer coalitions"; and boundary coalitions.

VERTICAL LINKS: HIERARCHIES

Many political actors are linked hierarchically: some by a clear status ordering of equals, superiors, and subordinates, some by a vertical chain of communication and command. Consider, for example, a political bureaucracy. Decisions at any one point in the bureaucracy may affect and be affected by other decisions in the hierarchical chain.

Applied to political hierarchies, Caplow's analysis yields some particularly clear and intriguing results. For one illustration, Caplow used a chain of "Type 5" triads in a hierarchical organization. This chain is shown in Figure 6.1, with the single lines representing the linkages between actors and the double lines the coalitions predicted. A Type 5 triad is the familiar case with $A > B > C$, $A < B + C$. Using only the two predictive principles, Caplow showed which coalitions will form in each triad and indicated a surprising consequence for the system as a whole. If a BC coalition forms to wrest power from A, player D has no choice but to form a coalition with E, thus winning in the CDE triad—and so on down the line. D might have preferred a DC coalition controlling B, but C prefers the BC coalition controlling A and cannot use B both as a partner and an opponent. In each triad, consequently, there would appear to be some revolutionary activity: B and C control the initially stronger A; D and E control the initially stronger C; and G and F control the initially stronger E. But, Caplow showed, looking at the system as a whole, much less of a revolution is apparent. The revolutionary coalitions formed in superior triads to seize power from the initially strongest actor become conservative coalitions in inferior triads *supporting the initial status order*. B and C dominate D, and D and E dominate F. The revolutionary activity does not in fact disrupt the hierarchy, but reorganizes it into three strata. The revolution may have toppled a leader, but all else remains the same.

A similar effect is shown for a chain of Type 2 triads ($A > B$, $B = C$, $A < B + C$) in Figure 6.2. Two equals can combine in a revolutionary co-

Figure 6.1 A Chain of Type 5 Triads

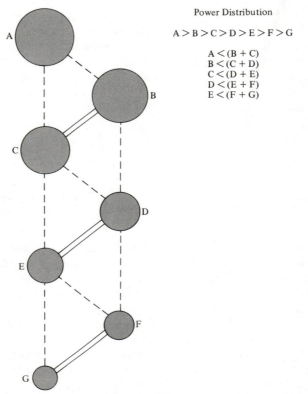

Power Distribution

A > B > C > D > E > F > G

$A < (B + C)$
$B < (C + D)$
$C < (D + E)$
$D < (E + F)$
$E < (F + G)$

A double line represents a coalition, a double line and two dotted lines represent a triad.

Source: Theodore Caplow, *Two Against One: Coalitions in Triads* (Englewood Cliffs, N.J.: Prentice-Hall, 1968), p. 58. © 1968. Reprinted by permission of Prentice-Hall, Inc.

alition against a stronger, but the coalition reinforces conservative coalitions in the inferior triads. Caplow commented:

> This figure presents a condition very often encountered in modern bureaucracy in which the power of individual superiors is greatly limited, solidarity among peers is much greater than that between superiors and subordinates, and peers call on each other for help in resisting authority and in coping with insubordination.[3]

Caplow diagramed linkages only for the Type 2 and Type 5 situations, commenting that a chain of Type 3 triads (A < B, B = C) would also maintain the initial status order. Type 3, in fact, taken outside Caplow's organi-

[3] Ibid., p. 61.

Figure 6.2   A Chain of Type 2 Triads

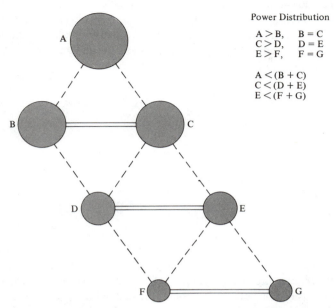

Power Distribution

A > B,   B = C
C > D,   D = E
E > F,   F = G

A < (B + C)
C < (D + E)
E < (F + G)

Source: Theodore Caplow, *Two Against One: Coalitions in Triads* (Englewood Cliffs, N.J.: Prentice-Hall, 1968), p. 61. © 1968. Reprinted by permission of Prentice-Hall, Inc.

zational context, is an intriguing case of a familiar international situation. Since B and C are equal and each alone is greater than A, a Type 3 chain is an inversion of Figure 6.2. Superpowers F and G are equal and greater than powers D and E, which are also equal and greater than small nations B and C, which are equal and greater than the tiny border country of A. The intriguing fact about the Type 3 chain is that whatever coalitions are formed, *the same order of power among the nations is preserved*. Following Caplow's two arguments, Nation E would be interested in a coalition with F or G, while G or F would want such a coalition only to stop each other from forming one. If coalition EG forms, coalition FD will form in defense, and so on down the line, at least through the BC case. Imagine, as in the diagram on the following page, an FDB coalition, say of communist nations, opposing an anticommunist GEC. Each coalition is equal: the nations have divided bilaterally (i.e., into two blocs), but the same order of power is maintained.

In this case, there may be trouble at the bottom of the system, causing A considerable uneasiness. Neither bilateral bloc may be able to afford to lose A to the other. Two satisfactory solutions from the standpoint of all the larger powers are to divide A in two or eliminate it from the situation. If A has the chance to bargain before the other alignments are made, such an event may be avoided. If A chooses either B or C as protector, other defensive coalitions are formed in response, the nations again dividing bilaterally. While the bloc that included A would have an advantage over the other in the entire system, any nation in any triad may be checked by the two others. (An EC coalition checks both F and D; an FD coalition checks both E and G.) In a situation of reciprocal checks and stalemates, the original order of power is maintained within and between triads.

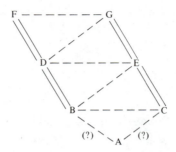

Alternately, if conservative coalitions form between equal powers, the original order of power among the nations is also maintained.

Thus we can link a particular coalition situation with a larger environment, show the interdependency of both, and ask how the various linkages contribute to the maintenance, reorganization, or overthrow of a complex order. Border disputes in A are of the keenest interest to F and G. Arms races and the proliferation of nuclear technology can be analyzed similarly. In Caplow's examples, there were only two predictive principles and the simplest structural framework; nevertheless, the social geometry hinted at is considerable. There are eight triadic types, some representing hierarchical and some nonhierarchical situations, and these can be linked in any number of combinations. Other principles and non-triadic forms could also be proposed. If, for example, some nations seek control of a coalition situation rather than the security of joining a superior coalition, different outcomes would be predicted.

HORIZONTAL LINKS: NOT SEPARATE BUT EQUAL

The vertical linkages of the organization chart can be extended to horizontal linkages as well. In the cases already discussed, choice of partner may be relatively simple. With the extension, any such choice in one vertical chain may conflict with a "peer coalition" in another chain.[4] Thus coalition activity in any one chain may affect and be affected by activity in another.

To take a political illustration, imagine that Figure 6.1 represents a bureaucratic segment organized around one policy area (for example, health)

[4] Ibid., pp. 130ff.

Figure 6.3   Three Possible Choices of Coalition Partner in a Linked Structure

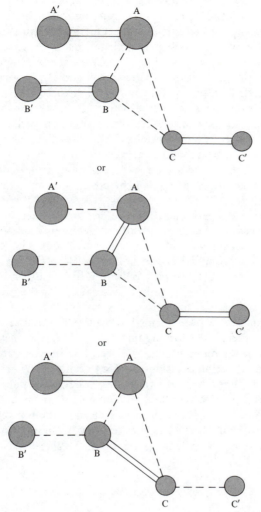

or

or

Source: Theodore Caplow, *Two Against One: Coalitions in Triads* (Englewood Cliffs, N.J.: Prentice-Hall, 1968), p. 131. © 1968. Reprinted by permission of Prentice-Hall, Inc.

with a parallel vertical chain organized around a second policy area (for example, energy) with both policy bureaucracies part of a larger bureaucratic structure. Actors A–G are engaged in coalition activity within their own hierarchy and with counterparts A_1–G_1 in another hierarchy. Bureaucrats B and B_1, concerned with health and energy policy respectively, may choose to compete for a portion of the budget, or they may choose to coordinate efforts to increase their autonomy from superiors or their control over subordinates. In other words, they are involved in multiple mixed-motive situations in which activity in any one affects activity in the others.

In Figure 6.3 Caplow presents one segment of such a complex linkage system, focusing on B's possible choices. Our health bureaucrat B may try to form a coalition with B_1 to protect their mutual interests against the powerful A–A_1 coalition; or a coalition with A to control C and protect their particular program against the activities of A_1 and B_1; or a coalition with C to check A in their own policy domain. None of these choices is necessarily inconsistent with Caplow's second principle of preference for a coalition in the superior triad. B may rationalize that a coalition with A would be the strongest. Because it would neutralize A_1, allow him to ignore B_1, and dominate C, B would be a member of a coalition in the most superior triad. But faced with the likelihood of an A–A_1 coalition, either choice of B_1 or C as coalition partner offers an equivalent coalition dominating A, either in the ABC triad or the ABB_1 triad.

It is clear that B's choice and the reciprocated choices of the other participants will affect (1) the strategy and the decisions made in any one triad and (2) the interworkings and interrelations of the "bureaucracy" as a whole. Assume that B, at a Latin American desk in the State Department, is unhappy with some U.S. foreign policy. Whether B can obtain information from C in the field, use B_1 to leak information to the press, or get a report passed up through A to a more powerful decision-maker will depend on what coalitions have been formed. Coalition formation will thus affect what policy is implemented for any one policy area, how it is implemented, and what the broader repercussions will be. The bureaucratic environment may be changed, affecting decision-making in both policy areas, from a vertical emphasis on hierarchy and a particular program or policy to a horizontal emphasis stratifying activity and personnel and cutting across programs. One can see the beginning of such stratification in the top representation in Figure 6.3. The original hierarchical order may be maintained or subverted. There may or may not be trouble at the top of the system or anywhere else.

BOUNDARY SITUATIONS

Beyond hierarchies, overlapping membership can take a number of different forms. Such familiar political practices as ex officio appointment, token representation, or the selection of advisers all create linked situations. One particular kind of linkage—the boundary situation—is particularly important and should be singled out for further attention. Caplow defined a boundary triad as consisting of two insiders in an organization and one outsider, representing another organization, with the two organizations in some interaction with each other.[5] In his example, the triad consisted of an account executive for an advertising company, his company, particularly as represented by its president, and a representative from the account company. By coordinating too much with his own company, the executive risked the loss of the account and loss of his job. But if he coordinated too much with the representative, he risked conflict with his own company and the loss of his job.

Unlike the multiple linkages described earlier, the boundary case focuses on a single linkage that is critical to both organizations and to the relationship between them. Caplow simply cited the example and indicated the problem. The boundary case, however, is worth more political attention.

We can extend the term *organization* to apply to any political institution, system, or bounded set of activity, and find many analogues for the account executive in the political world: a presidential press secretary, a labor leader active in a political party, or an army officer serving as consultant to a government. Nations, congressional subcommittees, and corporate economic interests can also form boundary coalitions.

The difficulties of department heads in the U.S. government are often due to the pressures of boundary situations. They are presidential appointees—thus members of the President's Cabinet—and simultaneously heads of departments composed of long-term civil service members. They are part of both the Presidency and the bureaucracy. So if they work too enthusiastically for the President's program, they risk isolation from the department; and if too enthusiastically for the department, isolation from the White House. For another example, consider the problem of "clientelism" in the foreign service—the tendency of bureaucrats confronting a conflict between the clients or interests they serve and the government employing them to side with the former; in other words, to join in coalition with their clients. Political scientist Roger Morris cited the case of one American foreign service officer assigned to an African nation who watched one tribe commit genocide on another. Bodies, said Morris, were carried past the embassy at the rate of 1000 a day, but the officer did not inform Washington for fear of hurting the country's relations with the United States and undermining the work he had been trying to do.[6]

Here is a mixed-motive situation of particular intensity, that challenges the use of political skills. In contrast to the account executive (who in fact lost his job), skillful political actors may turn boundary coalitions to considerable advantage. Subgovernments that form across private and public spheres are cases in point, with the members gaining economic profit and

---

[5] Ibid., p. 136.
[6] Roger Morris, "Rooting for the Other Team: Clientelism in the Foreign Service," in *Inside the System*, 3rd ed., ed. Charles Peters and James Fallows (New York: Praeger, 1976), pp. 171–81.

political influence from the situation. For another solution, some coalition behavior allows even those excluded from winning coalitions to see value in remaining in and repeating the coalition situation. The winners sacrifice some returns for the losers' consolation prize. For a third solution, boundary triads may maintain themselves by *not* forming coalitions. The communication and bargaining prior to coalition formation provide all actors with valuable information or symbolic support, and the subsequent decision not to form a coalition allows the process to repeat itself. And fourth, those actors with political sensitivity may be better able than Caplow's account executive to judge just how frequently one should form which coalitions, when one must form them and when one need not do so, and what the distribution of returns should be.

The point was raised in the preceding chapter that there are times when instability and unpredictability have value, when forging stable alliances is not the best strategy for the long term. Such appears to be the case in some boundary situations. Actors make known that they may or may not be available to form a coalition, and if they do join this time, they may not do so at another time. The very unpredictability becomes predictable, even "trustable." One remains available—and valuable—to all by forming a firm alliance with none.

Any of these solutions will in turn affect coalition formation throughout the linked organizations. Instability, strategies to accommodate losers, the choice of not forming coalitions or forming very strong and stable ones—all become key environmental factors for decisions made elsewhere.

Boundary coalitions are critical in defining the relations between any political organization and its environment. The particular kind of coalition activity at the boundaries between two political organizations affects coalition activity in each, and determines for any one such organization the extent to which it affects or is affected by its environment. The advantage of the kind of structural analysis suggested by Caplow is that focusing attention merely on such a boundary situation may tell us much about the organizations thus linked and what may be expected from the relationships between them.

OVERLAPPING MEMBERSHIP

Throughout this analysis, overlapping membership is highlighted as the critical factor. Any change, then, in this membership will initiate a whole series of changes along the various links in the chains. We can demonstrate this easily. Look back at Figure 6.1, and say that actor E, either by choice or necessity, begins to lose interest in CDE affairs to the extent that E, a member of the DEF triad, is no longer a member of CDE. (In other words, erase the dotted line between E and C.) E no longer needs D and may prefer a coalition with F dominating both D and G. If E succeeds in forming that coalition, one would find the situation as diagramed below:

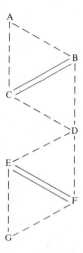

By a change merely in one actor's membership in one situation, the DE and FG coalitions dissolve, the EF coalition is formed, and D is effectively excluded from all influence within the hierarchy.

The effects of membership change are even clearer in the horizontal linkage shown in Figure 6.3. Civil Servant B's choice of coalition partner affects coalition activity in both vertical chains. If B leaves for a vice-presidency in industry, the next person to hold the job may choose a different coalition partner, initiating changes all along the line. And B's new job may create a new boundary situation between industry and bureaucracy, with B's personal connections acting as the link between what were two separate areas of political activity.

Who sets the membership and what processes determine its overlap therefore become major political questions. If linked structures are important in the ways indicated in this chapter, membership selection is equally important. These may be determined by noncoalitional processes—such as social opportunity, patterns of prejudice, or other socialization—or they may be determined by other coalitions.

One way, then, of seeing the relationship between political actors and their environment has been suggested by this discussion and is diagramed in Figure 6.4. The figure represents an expansion of one segment from Table 4.1. Presumably it could be extended to others.

The arrows in the diagram show the complex nature of the relationship. An actor engaged in the process of coalition formation (column three) works within an immediate environment of linked coalitions and a larger environment that reshapes the membership and its overlap. The coalitions formed from column three in turn affect the linked structure (column 2) and membership selection (column 1), as well as other outcomes. They de-

Figure 6.4 Environmental Effects and Three Dependent Variables: An Expanded Segment from Table 4.1

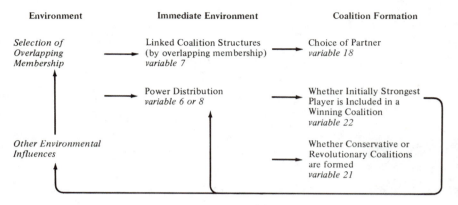

termine, for example, whether A is or is not included in a winning coalition, and whether coalitions will maintain or transform the status quo throughout the chain.

APPLICATION

Coalitions can be linked in any number of ways, activity in one situation affecting and being affected by activity in others. The structural analysis indicated in this chapter offers merely one way of addressing such linkages. Caplow's scheme can be applied directly or used to stimulate other more useful conceptualizations. It is, of course, easy to point out the limits of such an analysis. Caplow worked only with triads and with formal power among the actors, but politics is not always triadic or subject to formal status rankings. Perhaps more seriously, the scheme requires that overlapping membership be described and limited to a particular set of actors; otherwise, Figure 6.3 would expand indefinitely as everything becomes related, ultimately, to everything else.

Despite these limits, the idea suggests a number of potential applications. One could change the number of players or the goals or expand the predictive principles. Caplow assumed the goal of security: that players will seek the coalition with the largest total resources. But if players seek goals of efficiency or the control of the coalition, different outcomes would be predicted. The analysis might be clarified by the use of game theory or simplified by application to a particular case.

Robert Axelrod, for example, used both vertical and horizontal linkages in his analysis of multi-level decision making in bureaucracies.[7] His *Clear the Cable* game (see Chapter 4) begins with five actors and three bureaucratic levels:

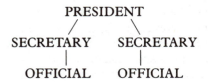

PRESIDENT

SECRETARY   SECRETARY

OFFICIAL   OFFICIAL

If the officials at either subpresidential level can agree, the cable is sent; if they cannot agree, the decision is referred to the higher level with a penalty for bothering the superior. We assume five different views of the most desired cable as well as calculation by the players of the value of their time, policy preference, and potential penalties. The problem quickly becomes very interesting.

Axelrod developed a game-theoretic model for analyzing the situation and showed how the model can be extended to additional levels of office (vertically) or additional agencies (horizontally). We can, for example, analyze the problem for two departments, three agencies, and twelve actors:

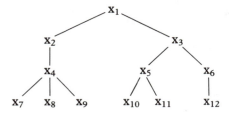

In other words, this structural analysis can be applied to a number of real-world political problems and is capable of translation to game theory. Using vertical and horizontal linkages, Axelrod specified a model for an *n*-person coalition game.

The chapter suggests the general point that simple structural relationships may help explain a number of political effects, such as the overthrow of leaders, the maintaining or altering of the status quo, and the return or redistribution of resources among the actors. These may be predicted for all combinations vertical or horizontal. By extension, we can explain other political effects: when, for instance, coalitions—in a government or an international system or a boundary triad—may be expected to persist, and when the stability of coalitions formed at one point will affect the stability somewhere else. More generally, we can begin to explain how coalition formation

---

[7] Robert Axelrod, *Conflict of Interest: A Theory of Divergent Goals with Applications to Politics* (Chicago: Markham, 1970), pp. 121–43.

in any one situation affects and is affected by coalition activity throughout the larger environmental chain.

Finally, the chapter suggests the potential for classifying political characteristics as structural effects. Caplow's eight triadic types may not be directly applicable, and the combination of types too numerous to be useful as an organizing device. Nevertheless, the discussion implies the possibility that major structural patterns could be identified and applied to politics. Superficially unlike things—governments, parties, international organizations—will exhibit like linkage structures producing like effects. Similar things—such as democratic regimes or developing nations—will need to be differentiated. Most disciplines have found structural classification a useful first step in ordering complex phenomena: political scientists, too, may find that structure is a powerful organizing device.

Just as coalitions need not be isolated in time, they need not be isolated in political space. The two chapters indicate that the simple framework initially introduced can be used to address complex political processes. The task of the following chapters is to show that it remains simple enough to use for empirical analysis.

III

Applications

The narrowing of focus in Part II now narrows further. We move to specific applications of the study of coalitions. Chapter 7 tests propositions about the effects of information on choice of coalition partner and illustrates how diverse studies can be accumulated and combined. Chapter 8 proposes some conceptual advantages of coalition analysis by defining party activity in legislatures. Chapter 9 suggests that coalition research can be combined with other developed political subject matters: in this case, the study of international alliances. These are illustrations, merely, but the range of subjects covered and of purposes addressed should indicate the breadth of possible application.

Chapter 7

Information and a Political Convention

One important theme developed in the earlier chapters is that the kind of information provided to the players can change coalition results. The social-psychological theories discussed in Chapter 2 could be reorganized according to the kind of information each provides. Some theories highlight single information cues in the players' initial distribution of resources; others highlight alternate cues; and others no clear cues. Later chapters examined such alternate cues as those provided by experience with the players, trust, and overlapping membership. It may now be asked more generally what happens when such alternate information is provided: specifically, *to what extent varying the kind of information (from single to alternate to no-clear-information cues) changes coalition behavior.*

The question has implications for a number of political situations in which information may change or be deliberately manipulated. Its importance for bandwagons and political conventions will be pursued in this chapter, but the implications should hold for a much wider range of political cases. We are asking how merely changing the kind of information available to the players can change the coalitions formed.

A "Political Decision Questionnaire" has been employed in studies designed to manipulate and test the effect of initial resources.[1] It may be reapplied and expanded to vary the kind of information provided. In the earlier experiments, subjects presented only with initial-resource cues tend-

---

[1] See, for example, James Phillips and Lawrence Nitz, "Social Contacts in a Three-Person 'Political Convention' Situation," *Journal of Conflict Resolution* 12 (June 1968): 206–14.

ed to choose players to bargain with who might help them form a minimum winning coalition; the initially strongest player was excluded. So it may be asked whether the same initial choice of bargaining partner will be found under the other two information conditions—or to what extent the fortunes of the initially strongest player vary under the three information conditions.

DESIGN

An experiment was designed to test the tendency to choose the initially strongest player (player A) under two different experimental conditions: the kind of information available; and the extent of player A's initial advantage.[2] The design varied the kind of information from single initial-resource cues to alternate cues to a situation in which no clear cues are available. It also varied A's initial lead in resources—from slight to strong to a decided lead that is not quite sufficient to win without forming a coalition. We could then test the effects of information across varying resource distributions. Thus in a situation with $A>B>C$, $A<B+C$, the subjects managing candidate C's campaign were asked whether A or B would be their first choice as bargaining partner.

Note that the question is limited to C's choice and does not test reciprocal choices. It is also limited to the initial choice of bargaining partner and not the final coalition formed. Hypothetically, if C chooses B, but B and A turn to each other, C's choice has no impact on the ultimate result. Even if C and B choose each other, the potential partnership may break down at the bargaining stage with one or both turning to initially excluded A. With these limits, no direct inferences may be made about outcomes; only the first step toward the outcome is measured. Nevertheless, first steps are often critical. Certainly A and B would care very much about C's answer and believe their chances strongly improved or reduced accordingly.

The subjects of the experiment were sixty-one juniors and seniors enrolled in an American National Government course at the University of Wisconsin, Madison. Students were asked to complete in class, with their names on the papers, a six-item Political Decision Questionnaire that would give them "the chance to test [their] own political decision-making abilities." The phrase is taken from the political decision experiment as tradi-

---

[2] The experiment reported in the chapter was published by the author in "The Effects of Information on Choice of Coalition Partner," *Experimental Studies of Politics* 6 (June 1977): 1–24.

tionally conducted. The cover sheet included with all the questionnaires read as follows:

Political Decision Questionnaire

Instructions

Assume you are the campaign manager for a candidate in a political party convention. There are a total of 100 votes among the delegates and at least a majority (51) of these are required to win the nomination. If no one candidate has enough votes to win alone, a *coalition* (e.g., between two candidates) must be formed with the members of the coalition deciding how to distribute *all* the winnings between them and the candidate not included in the coalition receiving *nothing*.

The rewards of winning may include the nomination itself, policy and issue additions and compromises between the two coalition members, preferment and access to the candidate who may finally win office in government. In other words, there are a number of "rewards" (psychic, social, as well as political and material) that can be divided between the coalition members and none of these are available to the one excluded from the coalition.

There are three candidates in the conventions you will be considering: Candidates "A," "B," and "C." You are campaign manager for Candidate C. In each of the following situations, you must decide which of the other two candidates—A or B—you will approach first to try to bargain to form a winning nominating coalition.

Recognize as you make this decision that the other two candidates face the same decision. They also will be deciding whom to approach first. And if they both choose each other, your candidate would lose (that is, would be excluded from the winning coalition).

The instructions highlighted the "winner-take-all" condition and the problem of reciprocal choices, thus putting people on notice that they were not alone in the game. It was felt that some students would recognize both problems immediately and intuitively, and that others would not; therefore attention was called to both conditions to make the choice as equivalent as possible for all. There had been no prior discussion in the class of coalitions or nominating conventions. At the completion of the questionnaire, students were asked to comment briefly on the reason for their choice in each case.

The initial-resource variable was measured on the questionnaire as follows. For candidates A, B, and C, respectively, one situation assigned a 49–30–21 delegate distribution, one situation a 45–35–20 distribution; and one a 38–35–27 distribution. The initially strongest Candidate A varied from a slight to a strong to a decided advantage, and the subject managing Candidate C's campaign had to choose between Candidate A or second-strongest Candidate B. These three items were used to measure the effect of initial resources in the experiment. The remaining three items on the questionnaire simply gave people the chance to look at some of the same distributions from the perspective of A and B and were used so as not to overfocus attention on the experimental-resource variable.

A's decided lead of 49 delegate votes is not sufficient to win. Hypothetically, a BC coalition can form to exclude A—in the experiment, in a convention hall, or in any other political situation. So the extent to which B or C recognize at this point that they need not rush to join A's bandwagon is of some considerable interest. The perception may be "incorrect" that A cannot be stopped, but it is the perception—not some hypothetically correct answer—that will affect choice of partner.

The second variable employed in the experiment was the information condition: varying the situation from one of single clear resource cues, to one of alternate and competing cues, to one in which no clear cues were provided. Three forms of the questionnaire were constructed paralleling these three information conditions, with the subjects randomly assigned to one of the three conditions. All three forms of the questionnaire included the same three items measuring the initial-resource variable. Questionnaire #1 supplied only initial resource cues for all items. It paralleled the earlier experiments using this device. Questionnaire #2 supplied identical information on resources, but added the alternate and contradictory cue that Candidate B was considered the favorite. Questionnaire #3 gave no clear information. A delegate poll was provided reporting resource distributions identical to the other two questionnaires, but it was stressed that the poll was nonbinding and the delegates were shifting rapidly. Other poll and primary information was included, deliberately balanced to confuse the relative status of A and B.

To illustrate, the following situations were used in each of the three questionnaire forms for the 45–35–20 resource distribution:

Questionnaire #1—one clear cue.

In this convention, with 51 votes necessary to win, your candidate, Candidate C, has 20 votes pledged. Candidate A has 45 votes and Candidate B has 35 votes. Which of the other two candidates, A or B, will you approach first to try to bargain with to form a winning nominating coalition?

A   B   (circle one)

Questionnaire #2—alternate cues

In this convention, with 51 votes necessary to win, Candidate B has been considered the favorite. Going into the convention, your candidate, Candidate C, has 20 votes pledged. Candidate A has 45 votes and Candidate B has 35 votes. Which of the other two candidates A or B, will you approach first to try to bargain with to form a winning nominating coalition?

A   B   (circle one)

Table 7.1 Choice of Partner Under Three Information Conditions: Number of Subjects Choosing A or B

INITIAL RESOURCE DISTRIBUTION (A's INITIAL LEAD)	ONE CLEAR CUE (N = 20)		ALTERNATE CUES (N = 21)		NO CLEAR CUES (N = 20)		SIGNIFICANCE[a]
	A	B	A	B	A	B	
Decided (49–30–21)	11	9	9	12	15	5	$p < .05$
Strong (45–35–20)	7	13	11	10	12	8	n.s.
Slight (38–35–27)	5	15	9	12	14	6	$p < .05$

[a] Level of significance for one-tailed test; chi square, 2 df.

Questionnaire #3—no clear cues

In this convention with 51 votes necessary to win, no candidate has emerged as a primary winner (in fact, all three have done rather badly). There are no favorites. The latest delegate poll shows 20 delegates expressing a preference for your candidate, Candidate C. 45 express a preference for Candidate A and 35 for Candidate B. These preferences could change and are in no way binding. Which of the other two candidates, A or B, would you approach first to try to bargain with to form a winning nominating coalition?

A   B   (circle one)

Many variations were used in Questionnaire #3 for the different items. One described a situation where "the primaries are split and the polls are shifting rapidly." Another pointed out that "all candidates have won some primaries (though B made a stronger showing than expected and A has just won the California primary)." While the details varied, each item was designed to give no clear information as to the relative strength of A and B. (An additional item was included in Questionnaire #3 to tap a very specific information condition, which will be discussed in a later section.)

RESULTS

The results are summarized in Tables 7.1 and 7.2. Table 7.1 reports the frequency of choice of A or B for the three resource distributions and the three information conditions. Table 7.2 translates these frequencies into the players' "chance" of being chosen: that is, whether they appear advantaged, disadvantaged, or faced with an even chance under the various conditions. Choice of A or B can be tested against chance under the binomial distribu-

Table 7.2 Probabilities of C Choosing Either A or B[a]

A'S INITIAL LEAD	ONE CLEAR CUE (N = 20)	ALTERNATE CUES (N = 21)	NO CLEAR CUES (N = 20)
Decided (49–30–21)	.824	.664	.042 (A)
Strong (45–35–20)	.264 (B)	.999	.504
Slight (38–35–27)	.042 (B)	.664	.116 (A)

[a] Probabilities of C choosing either A or B, against a distribution resulting from chance, under the binomial distribution, one-tailed, from the frequencies reported in Table 7.1. When the probabilities clearly diverge from chance, the letters in parenthesis report the player "advantaged" in the choice.

tion for N's from 5 to 25.[3] Table 7.2 reports these probabilities. The larger the number, the more closely we can say it approximates a tossup (chance) situation; the smaller the number, the more likely (against chance) either A or B will tend to be chosen, and is thus advantaged by the situation.

The tables taken together provide some initial support for the importance of information effects. Candidate A is disadvantaged under the first information condition, where only initial resource cues are provided. This repeats the result of earlier experiments. As A gains in initial resources to the point of approaching victory, subjects are less likely to disregard A in favor of a minimum win. Still, under the best of circumstances—and a "decided" lead in delegate votes—A faces a tossup situation.

The postexperimental comments divided between two different perceptions of the situation for this first information condition: the majority perceiving the advantages of a minimum winning coalition, and the others the advantages of being with the front-runner. Typical comments included the following:

On minimum win perceptions:

> I chose the other candidate whose votes, when added to mine, would add up closest to a 51-vote total. I thought the less number of people in the coalition the better.

> I felt I had less to lose and would have to compromise less by joining with the second-highest vote getter.

On front-runner perceptions:

> Either candidate we form a coalition with will have more votes than we do. I picked A since he is the stronger candidate.

> B gives no safety margin . . . A is the safer choice, ensuring victory.

[3] See, for example, Sidney Siegel, *Nonparametric Statistics for the Behavioral Sciences* (New York: McGraw-Hill, 1956), pp. 36–42.

No subjects on this first play of the game articulated their own "pivotal power" position: the fact that they were as important as either B or A to a winning coalition and thus in an equally strong bargaining situation.

With alternate and competing cues, A faces a tossup whatever the distribution of resources. This is particularly important where the resource advantage is slight, for by the addition of one contradictory piece of information, A's chances improve from a tendency not to be chosen to a fairly even chance. The postexperimental comments for this information condition also divided between minimum win and front-runner perceptions, but there was further division as to who was the front-runner. Some saw the favorite as the stronger and others the leader in delegate votes.

Under the third information condition, with no clear cues, player A's situation improves markedly. At the extreme, with a slight initial lead, A's situation has changed from a strong tendency not to be chosen to a strong tendency to be chosen. Comparing columns one and three in Table 7.1 for the slight advantage condition, the number of subjects choosing A or B are almost exactly reversed. Under the decided initial-lead condition, A has improved from a tossup to a strong tendency to be chosen.

The majority of subjects under this third information condition chose the frontrunner because they saw Player A as "the best bet to win," "the most likely to win," "the stronger of the two—every vote may count," or in more detail:

> I chose A with the polls showing he had a commanding lead. I felt a coalition with B in that case was cutting it too close, considering our coalition might lose votes to A, leaving us both compromised and losers.

A number of other subjects, however, omitted giving any rationale or explained there was "no real choice," "no good choice," "it doesn't matter which," echoing Gamson's prediction of random choice under such confused conditions (see Chapter 2). Only a few subjects still opted, under this information condition, for a try at a minimum win.

Overall, choice of partner appears affected by the kind of information provided, with the initially strongest player more advantaged as information is added and confused. The results for Table 7.1 are significant ($p<.05$) for the slight and the decided advantage conditions. The same tendency appears for the strong advantage condition, although the result is not significant at the .05 level. This discrepancy will be discussed later in more detail. Table 7.2 indicates further how information affects the chances of the initially strongest player—with a decided lead, from tossup to advantage; with a strong lead, from disadvantage to tossup; and with a slight lead, from disadvantage to advantage. In contrast, the size of A's initial lead appears to have little effect. Only under the single-cue condition does the size of the lead affect A's chances. Under the other two conditions, A remains in a tossup or receives no consistent advantage or disadvantage.

Table 7.3 Information and Choice of Partner: *The New York Times* **Declares a Frontrunner**

	NUMBER OF SUBJECTS	
QUESTIONNAIRE ITEM[a]	C Chooses A	C Chooses B
A leads in polls (38–35–27; no clear cues)	14	6
A leads in polls (38–35–27; *Times* calls B the "frontrunner")	6	14

[a] Twenty subjects completed Questionnaire #3, which included these two items. Chi square = 4.9, p<.05, two-tailed, 1 df.

The New York Times Declares a Front-runner

There is one additional finding deserving attention. One item was included in Questionnaire #3 reporting that "*The New York Times* calls B the 'front-runner'." The resource distribution used was identical to another item in that questionnaire in which A had the slight advantage of a 38–35–27 lead in the delegate polls. One may thus compare the impact of the *Times* report for the same resource distribution and the same otherwise-unclear information condition. ("The delegate preferences could change and are in no way binding. The polls and primaries show mixed results . . .")

The results are shown in Table 7.3. With the *Times* report, A's fortunes changed dramatically. C's tended to choose *Times* "front-runner" B over A in exactly reverse proportions, with chi square results significant at the .05 level. With the news, A's chances turned around. No other circumstance had changed at all.

Some subjects appeared to take the *Times* report directly as an expression of B's strength, as shown in the following postexperimental rationales:

> It's nice to be with the front-runner as expressed by a major paper.

> Assuming the *N.Y. Times* as a fairly credible source, B appears to be gaining strength. A coalition with B could prove to be successful.

> As long as candidates A and B are so close I'd choose B—*The Times* may know something I don't.

> [or simply] Candidate B seems more likely to win.

Others were less impressed by the report per se than by the fact that the publicity would impress others. "I chose B," said one, because "The delegates may be influenced by the publicity." Another felt "The publicity could sway more [delegates] for B," and a third said that "The influence of the media is worth a lot." One person reacted negatively to the same information and chose A over B. Said this independent Midwesterner: "The *Times* position alone, which may be viewed as endorsement, would induce me to pick A. . . ." However it was viewed, the report tended to be taken as the only clear piece of information in an otherwise confused situation.

DISCUSSION

There is some evidence, then, that coalition behavior will change with the kind of information available to the actors. Initially strongest A tends not to be chosen, faces an even chance, or tends to be chosen depending on whether single, alternate, or no clear cues are provided. This effect, moreover, can be observed with varying degrees of strength for the different initial-resource conditions. At its clearest, with a slight initial lead, A's fortunes are reversed from a strong disadvantage to an equal chance to a strong advantage, depending on the information provided. With the addition of one fact to the poor information condition—the fact that *The New York Times* calls B the front-runner—A's fortunes are reversed again as the subjects move to join the *Times* front-runner.

If the result holds under further testing, the strategic implications are considerable. Merely changing the kind of information, where this is possible for political actors, may change the tendency of one versus other kinds of coalitions to form. Other things equal, A's best strategy is clear from Tables 7.1 and 7.2. Adding information avoids a loss; creating confusion brings victory. Player B, on the other hand, would want things as clear and simple as possible in order to encourage a lucid, cool-thinking, unpanicked C. Apparently neutral arrangements—for the size of the convention hall, the communication facilities available, the number of speeches and demonstrations permitted—can help one candidate more than another.

Information, of course, can be changed by others outside the coalition situation. The role of the news media, for example, in presidential nominating politics has been the subject of widespread concern, shared by the media representatives themselves. Candidates are declared in and out of races; front-runners are called; primary results are given different interpretations. The experiment underscores these worries, reversing the choice of partner by declaring a front-runner. In *actual* presidential nominations, those declared front-runners by *The New York Times* on the eve of the convention, before any balloting, are overwhelmingly likely to win the nomination.[4] This may appear uninteresting: the *Times* merely reports a "fact," or a strong potential, which awaits fulfillment. In the experiment, however, there was no "fact" existing independently of the report, and yet similar re-

[4] Barbara Hinckley, "The Initially Strongest Player: Coalition Games and Presidential Nominations," *American Behavioral Scientist* 18 (March/April 1975): 497–512. See also Chapter 2.

sults were seen. While the experiment is a considerable simplification of any political reality, it does serve to isolate the effect of this one journalistic cue. If political actors, like experimental subjects, are impressed by what they read in the paper *or* believe that others will be impressed by what they read in the paper, then the experiment can help dramatize this major public concern.

In addition, these results can clarify the questions about bandwagons raised in earlier chapters, taking bandwagons to be represented by the choice of the initially strongest player as "the best bet to win." Two findings are of interest. First, the tendency to form bandwagons was affected by the kind of information available: least likely with single clear resource cues, most likely with no good information of any kind. Secondly, the extent of A's advantage in initial resources appeared to have little effect on bandwagon formation. For two of the information conditions, no effect was discernible; for the other, A improved to a tossup, hardly what one could call a bandwagon effect.

The results also suggest a number of follow-up questions. Player B's choice and reciprocal choices were not measured. Outcomes would be changed by the other players' reactions to the various information. Two kinds of strategies were observed, categorized as minimum winning and front-runner perceptions. Why subjects chose these two very different strategies is also worth pursuing. Subjects may have different perceptions about the game, different experience with other like situations, or different tendencies to take high-risk or low-risk options. Experience with the game appears particularly important. Subjects choosing A as the most likely to win—given the first information condition—were "incorrect" in that A could not win without forming a coalition. More experience with the game might change that perception, thus benefiting B, *or* might lead other subjects to appreciate that some of their members make "incorrect" judgments, thus benefiting A.

The effects of the poor information condition are particularly intriguing, in view of past speculation on the subject. Gamson suggested such a condition may lead to random choice. The present results suggest the alternative of an advantage to the initially strongest player. In the absence of any good information, any cue no matter how unreliable may be decisive—even the tenuous, shifting lead in the delegate polls. Nevertheless, there is some support for both predictions. While a majority of subjects chose A as "the best bet to win," a number of others pointed out there was "no good choice" and may well have been choosing randomly. Random choice helps explain the anomaly in the strong-advantage condition as shown in Table 7.1. At least there appears no other clear reason why A would tend to be chosen with a "decided" and a "slight" advantage and not with the advantage between these two extremes. Table 7.2 summarizes the mixed evidence on the point. It is true that A tends to be advantaged under poor information for two of the three resource distributions, and is not advantaged at any point under the other two information conditions. Yet it is also true that accepting a significance level as large as .05 for rejecting chance, we are only able to reject it—to reject random choice—for one of the cases under poor information. The question is worth more study in similar and other kinds of "confused" conditions. The scenes of bedlam Gamson described were not approximated in the experiment. It may be that the more confused the condition for choice, the more likely actors would choose randomly.

We have, then, a simple experimental design which could be employed for many follow-up questions. The results can be expanded by questions about experience with the game, extent of confusion in the situation, other players' choices. It should be particularly interesting to see how differences in experience—with the game itself or with other strategic situations—affect results. Other variables from earlier chapters could also be introduced. While the design is simple to administer and fun to play, it is capable of accumulating and classifying a large amount of coalition research.

Experiments, we said earlier, can offer a valuable supplement to political research. Both the possibilities and limits of the technique should now be clearer. We cannot generalize directly to political conventions from the experimental design, but we can isolate, and clarify the effects of, factors of direct importance: the effects of information, journalistic cues, conditions for bandwagons, or random choice. Studies of actual presidential nominations show that front-runners are advantaged by a self-fulfilling prophecy whereby the candidates who win are those who are perceived as most likely to win. These studies, however, have difficulty isolating the contributory conditions. Experiments can more easily isolate such conditions, but cannot assert that any particular condition approximates the actual nominating situation. Studies of presidential nominations are severely limited in the number of cases for analysis. With nominations once in four years, a full century is required to yield fifty cases from the two major parties. The more precise the historical controls imposed on the analysis, the smaller the number of cases. An N of 10 does not inspire the use of many control variables. On the other hand, presidential nominations represent an event of major importance and very high stakes which is at best only weakly simulated in any experiment. Within these limits, tendencies to choose front-runners—or any other nominating coalition effects—can be better understood by a convergence of these approaches than by either alone.

Game theorists have also studied bandwagons and other aspects of nominating coalition formation. Some of the studies combine formal models with descriptions of actual nominating cases.[5] As the examples in Chapter 2 demonstrate, all three approaches can be employed, either alone or in combination, for a fuller analysis of the subject.

Coalition analysis should help the accumulation and organization of diverse political information. For *any* political situation, we may be interested in how changes in information can change bargaining and results. Or we

---

[5] John Aldrich, *Before the Convention* (Chicago: University of Chicago Press, 1980); and Steven Brams, *The Presidential Election Game* (New Haven: Yale University Press, 1978).

may be interested in the conditions helping or hurting the initially strongest player in maintaining control of a coalition situation. This player might be a would-be dictator, a party with a plurality of legislative seats, or any other resource leader in a political situation. Hence, the results from this chapter can be added to other studies addressing these subjects. Previous chapters have cited work on joining or blocking political bandwagons,[6] the tendency in cumulative games to unite against the leader,[7] and strategies for evading dictatorial control.[8] An Apex Game has been analyzed in which players must choose between cooperating with the leader or forming a unanimous alliance of all the weaker players.[9] (The leader is the apex; all the weaker players are the base.) One study of the Apex Game employed a selective incentive system, so that the base players could penalize any of their members who attempted to bargain with the leader, and identified conditions under which coalitions blocking the leader could be increased.[10] All of these studies, characterized by diverse approaches and substantive expertise, can together address such important political questions.

SUMMARY

The chapter focused on the effects of information on coalition choice and suggested that minimum winning choices may be contingent upon the kind of information provided. If the only cue provided by the situation is initial resources, B and C will choose each other simply because there is no good reason to do otherwise. Initial resources, then, should have no special status in coalition theory, but be merely one kind of information that can be used

---

[6] See especially Steven Brams and Jose Garriga-Pico, "Bandwagons in Coalition Formation," *American Behavioral Scientist* 18 (March/April 1975): 472–96; Steven Brams and J. Heilman, "When to Join a Coalition, and with How Many Others, Depends on What You Expect the Outcome to Be," *Public Choice* 17 (Spring 1974): 11–26; James Zais and John Kessel, "A Theory of Presidential Nominations with a 1968 Illustration," in *Perspectives on Presidential Selection*, ed. Donald Matthews (Washington, D.C.: Brookings, 1973), pp. 120–42; Philip Straffin, Jr., "The Bandwagon Curve," *American Journal of Political Science* 21 (November 1977): 695–709.

[7] P. Hoffman et al., "Tendencies Toward Group Comparability in Competitive Bargaining." *Human Relations* 7 (May 1954): 141–59; Jerome Chertkoff, "Sociopsychological Views on Sequential Effects in Coalition Formation," *American Behavioral Scientist* 18 (March/April 1975): 451–71.

[8] Bruce Bueno de Mesquita and Richard Niemi, "A Dynamic Theory of Coalition Formation," (Paper delivered at the Midwest Political Science Association Meeting, Chicago, April 1980).

[9] Abraham Horowitz and Amnon Rapoport, "Test of the Kernel and Two Bargaining Set Models in Four- and Five-Person Games," in *Game Theory as a Theory of Conflict Resolution*, ed. Anatol Rapoport (Boston: D. Reidel, 1974), pp. 161–92.

[10] Pamela Oliver, "Selective Incentives in an Apex Game," *Journal of Conflict Resolution* 24 (March 1980): 113–41.

in choosing coalition partners. Attention must be directed to the kind of information provided and to the conditions under which it will be considered. Attention must also be directed to the range of conditions under which resource leaders can be disadvantaged or supported. The results of experimental work may have considerable political relevance if it is true that merely manipulating the information provided changes a player's tendency to win or lose and helps shape the composition of a winning coalition.

Chapter 8

Defining Party Activity in Legislatures

Coalition activity, we have said, supplies a definition of political activity. The conceptual advantages of such a definition are both obvious and important. We can begin to classify and relate diverse political things and identify likeness and unlikeness beyond superficial characteristics. "Special" subjects, treated in isolation, can be reanalyzed and reappraised. Hence, a coalition framework can do more than accumulate and extend the analysis of political events; it can clarify the very concepts we use for such an analysis. This chapter supplies one illustration of these conceptual possibilities for the subject of political parties.

THE PROBLEM OF CONCEPTUALIZATION

Parties are widely claimed to be central to democratic processes. Writers for more than a century have stressed the critical place of parties in linking the mass public with a governing elite, worried that American parties were not strong (or "responsible") enough, tried to show they "make a difference" in all branches and levels of government, and are now concerned with their decline and realignment. Yet, with all the writing on the subject, there remains a problem of definition. We do not know what this thing is we are claiming to be important and so do not know (1) what we should or should not be linking it to and (2) what we should be comparing its importance against.

We assume that parties link separate phenomena that happen to share the same name. There are Republicans in the Congress, in the state legislatures and courts, and among the voters. "Partyness" in the executive links "partyness" in the legislature: having a president of the same party helps the party in Congress. In the same fashion, "partyness" in the electorate links up with "partyness" in the legislature: increasing the number of partisans elected increases the activity or success of the party in Congress. But we have no way of testing these linkages because we have not identified alternative possible influences: we have not compared party legislative activity to some other equivalent kind of legislative activity. If we do not know what it is, we cannot compare it to other like things. We need, in short, to take party outside of itself and define it in terms of a larger frame of political reference.

A coalition framework provides one solution to this problem of definition. Coalitions are ways of organizing political resources: in the standard definition, "the joint use of resources to determine the outcome of a decision in a mixed-motive situation." Parties are, specifically, one way of organizing political resources in such situations. They may be seen, then, as *one kind of coalition that can be compared against others and analyzed within the larger coalition frame.*

Thinking of a party as a coalition allows us first to see it as merely one of a number of possible coalitions, and thus to compare its performance against others. It is assigned no special status at the outset. If we are studying parties in legislative settings, we can compare the occurrence of party coalitions against other kinds of coalitions. Or if we are looking at the decline or realignment of legislative parties, we can compare such occurrences over time. Realignment might be seen as a change in coalition partner. So to assess the "importance" of party, we can compare party coalition activity against other coalition activity and against a no-coalition result. To assess stability, we can compare the relative frequency of this activity over time.

This conceptualization also suggests a number of questions about when and under what conditions party activity should be important. We can hypothesize when one kind of coalition would form as opposed to others: when, for example, changes in resources, stakes, or ideological distance predict the outcome. To explain party activity in legislatures, we can ask how differences in repetition or experience with the other coalition actors change results. Legislatures differ widely in the experience and stability of their membership, in rules governing bargaining, and in political stakes. They differ in the length of their sessions and in the number of cases requiring controversial decisions. All of these differences can be seen as independent variables affecting coalition results.

Say, for example, we wish to examine the effect of such external influences as executives or election results on legislative coalition activity. Material from an earlier chapter supplies a specific proposition on the point. Coalition behavior should differ in single and repetitive games (Chapter 5).

We have seen the following as important in repetitive coalition situations: learned behavior about the players and about the game, the development of trust, accumulated resource or status rankings, attitudes toward persistent winners and losers. Thus the importance of initial resource distribution may give way in repetitive games to the importance of accumulated status rankings. The importance of trust in maintaining a stable alliance may lead to a choice of partner not predicted by initial resources. The rules of the game may be adapted or added to (for example by legislative norms) through the learned behavior of the players. The result in all these cases is that the initial external influences, of major importance in single games, are reduced in importance through the repetition of play.

When the argument is applied to legislative parties, it raises questions about their linkage with other party phenomena outside the coalition situation. It suggests that legislative coalition activity would be more or less independent of such phenomena depending on the degree the particular legislature approximated a repetitive situation: that is, in terms of its stability of membership, length and continuity of session, and frequency of cases calling for coalition formation. At the extreme of repetition, one would find a kind of "impermeability" to external influences—an independence of them—because the players would be primarily constrained by the strategies, past results, and future expectations developed over the course of play.

The argument could be applied comparatively or used as a basis against which to interpret any one legislative result. External events could include election results (the initial resource distribution for legislative coalition formation) or any issue affecting government raised by events in the world outside the legislative halls. For legislatures with independently selected executives, the activity of the executive would also be considered an "external" event. We might thus expect in repetitive situations that the frequency of party coalition activity versus non-party coalition activity or no coalition activity would not vary with such events and that the frequency would be pervasive across issues. Coalitions formed or re-forming in one area would tend to do so in all areas, the pervasiveness of the pattern indicating independence from any particular external events.

This chapter explores the usefulness of the conceptualization. It is applied to one party in one legislature: the Democratic Party in the U.S. House of Representatives. In its stability of membership and number of cases posing controversial decisions, the House represents an ideal case of repetitive coalition activity. The illustrative nature of the application should be clear at the outset. What is done for House Democrats, with a particular set of definitions and measures, can be done elsewhere and measured differently. The point is to show that it can be done—that parties can be conceptualized as part of a larger political universe, be compared to non-party coalitions, and be analyzed for specific effects. Therefore, the primary purpose of the chapter is conceptual and not empirical. We cannot "test" the hypothesis with one example—although we can offer a case in support.

What we can do is work through—for one legislature and one argument—how the subject of parties might be approached through coalition analysis, and some of the problems that need to be faced along the way.

PROBLEMS OF MEASUREMENT

Applying coalition analysis to legislatures raises the problems of measurement discussed in Chapter 3. We need to consider when a coalition situation may be said to occur, who are the relevant coalition players, and what can be assumed about their goals in the situation. We also need to identify some universe of cases that will allow us to distinguish between a case of coalition formation and a no-coalition result. The following design indicates one approach to these questions.

Each coalition situation is here represented by one controversial roll call vote (to be explained below). We can assume congressional coalition actors care about the legislation being decided by roll calls, that they see themselves as engaged in a series of such situations, and that they seek to maximize their success over time. While some roll calls will be more important than others, such differences may be expected to cancel each other over time.

Restricting the cases to controversial roll calls is necessary to accord with the stipulation of some element of conflict in a coalition game. Near-unanimous roll calls may or may not represent the outcome of a coalition situation. They may be the aftermath of an earlier coalition or there may never have been an element of conflict in the situation at all. It is also true that coalitions may form in committee, in informal meetings of leaders, or at other stages of the legislative process—none of which are recorded by a controversial roll call vote. Restricting the analysis to controversial roll calls holds to the definition of a coalition by allowing the after-the-fact recognition that some coalition situation has occurred and keeps the study manageable, but it should be recognized that it taps only one portion of the wider coalition activity occurring in Congress.

While a number of different conceptualizations of coalition actors are possible, three are of particular interest for congressional parties. These are the blocs of Northern Democrats (ND), Southern Democrats (SD), and Republicans (R), with the South defined as the eleven states of the Confederacy. Several reasons can be cited for the usefulness of this selection. The blocs are well-known and commonly recognized as important in congressional politics. They are sufficiently active across the range of legislation so that analyzing this particular triad allows us to analyze virtually all House controversial roll-call activity. Finally, the selection allows us to examine the frequency of party coalitions (ND + SD) compared against nonparty coalitions (either SD + R or ND + R) or no coalition activity. The conservative coalition is a joining of Southern Democrats with Republicans—in other words SD + R. We thus gain a comparative measure, for the particular Democratic party coalition, of its "importance" compared to other coalition activity and of any change in relative importance over time or with varying presidential party conditions.

Can we, then, assume consciousness and coordination for these three blocs as coalition actors? According to a large literature on the subject, the three blocs exhibit internal communication, acknowledged leadership, and distinct legislative goals. A rich case literature details the efforts of a civil rights coalition (ND + R), a case of trading wheat for food stamps (ND + SD), or the orchestrated defeat of an education bill (SD + R). While overt coordination between and within blocs need not be assumed, we can assume reasonably good communication and information among the actors, and so at least the conditions for tacit coordination. Documentation of excellent information on voting possessed by the leadership,[1] the stability of members' voting on particular issues over time,[2] and the tacit and sometimes overt coalition activity engaged in by Southern Democrats and Republicans,[3] provide additional support for the assumption.

Measuring such activity, however, raises an additional difficulty. On the one hand, we need to distinguish coalition activity as much as possible from an accidental conjunction of individual members. Since one can vote only yes or no (if one votes at all), a majority of two blocs can vote together with no consciousness or coordination involved in doing so. There would be no awareness of joining resources to determine outcomes. Thus a *majority definition* of coalition activity (more than 50 percent of the members of each of two blocs voting together) is open to question. On the other hand, a *unanimity definition* (100 percent of each bloc voting together) is unrealistic and overstates the necessary assumptions. Leaders mobilize their own bloc's resources and coordinate with another bloc's leadership without expecting a perfect response. Individual defections are always assumed. Accepting some cut-off point between a majority and a unanimity has the disadvantage of appearing arbitrary and yet the advantage of making it easier to infer that some conscious activity and mobilization of resources have occurred. The rule adopted here was to define such activity halfway between the two extremes. It required that three-fourths or more of a bloc's voting members vote together with another similarly defined bloc—which implies that some mobilization of resources, either tacit or overt, has occurred. An alternative measure, based on the majority definition, can corroborate the results. The

[1] Randall Ripley, "The Party Whip Organizations in the United States House of Representatives," *American Political Science Review* 58 (1964): 561–676.
[2] Aage Clausen, *How Congressmen Decide* (New York: St. Martin's Press, 1973).
[3] John Manley, "The Conservative Coalition in Congress," *American Behavioral Scientist* 17 (November/December 1974): 223–347.

empirical fact in the House case is that both measures show the same results.

We can, then, define a bloc's "activity" as cases in which 75 percent or more of its voting members vote on one side, and "coalition" as cases in which 75 percent or more of each of two blocs are on the same side. Roll calls in which at least 75 percent of each of the three blocs are on the same side are called noncontroversial and are excluded from the analysis. The definitions are based on members present and voting.[4]

In a series of earlier studies, these definitions were applied to controversial roll calls in the House from the 85th through the 91st congresses (1957 through 1970).[5] We can use the results of that analysis for the present illustration. The congresses all show Democratic Party control of the House from the extremely narrow margin of the 85th to the overwhelming majority of the 89th. They span four different presidential administrations from Eisenhower through Nixon: two Republican and two Democratic. We can, then, examine coalition activity across time and across issues and under varying presidential-party conditions. Specifically, we can examine the "importance" and "decline" of the Democratic Party coalition compared to other coalitions and then the extent to which House coalition activity, including party coalition activity, is linked to varying presidential-party effects. The time period, it will be seen, is critical in revealing a change in House coalition partners.

PARTY ACTIVITY AS COALITION ACTIVITY

What is the importance of party activity in a legislature compared to other coalition activity, and what changes in importance can be identified? Measuring importance by the relative frequency of occurrence of one coalition

---

[4] Controversial roll calls by this definition comprise from approximately half to more than two-thirds of all House roll calls. For the seven congresses of the study, the results were as follows:

	85th	86th	87th	88th	89th	90th	91st
N controversial roll calls	136	137	159	140	223	253	184
N all roll calls	188	180	240	232	394	478	443
Percent controversial roll calls	72	76	65	60	57	53	42

The number of controversial roll calls tended to increase through the time period, but the number of noncontroversial roll calls has increased more sharply; thus the declining percentages.

[5] See Barbara Hinckley, "Coalitions in Congress: Size in a Series of Games," *American Politics Quarterly* 1 (July 1973): 339–59, and " 'Stylized' Opposition in the House of Representatives," *Legislative Studies Quarterly* 2 (February 1977): 5–28.

Table 8.1   Frequency of Coalition Activity: House Controversial Roll Calls, 85th–91st Congresses (1957–1970)

CONGRESS	85th	86th	87th	88th	89th	90th	91st
ACTIVITY[a]	PERCENT OF ALL CONTROVERSIAL ROLL CALLS						
Coalition activity occurs							
Two blocs active on the same side	40	45	53	41	31	37	34
No coalition activity occurs							
One bloc active or two blocs active on opposing sides	56	51	41	59	69	61	60
No bloc active	4	4	6	0	0	2	6
(N)	136	137	159	140	223	253	184

[a] Includes all possibilities. Cases where these blocs are active on the same side are defined as "noncontroversial" and excluded from the analysis.

compared to others, we can gain some answers for House Democrats from Tables 8.1 and 8.2.

Coalitions and No Coalitions

Table 8.1 shows the place of House coalition activity within all controversial roll call decisions. Since the decision not to form a coalition is as worthy of study as the decision to form one, the table can help identify the relative frequency of these outcomes. Employing the 75 percent definition, coalitions occur between one-third and one-half of the time (row one). If we had employed a majority definition, virtually 100 percent of the roll calls would show coalition activity: two of the three blocs, except for even splits within blocs, would always be found on one side. Employing the present 75 percent definition, then, appears helpful in discriminating the kinds of activity occurring. Note that there are very few cases in which no blocs are active in the controversial decisions (see row three), but in many cases, a bloc is not able to form a coalition with another (row two). By this measure, coalition activity among the three blocs is a frequent but by no means predomi-

Table 8.2 House Coalition Activity: 85th–91st Congresses

CONGRESS	85th	86th	87th	88th	89th	90th	91st
PRESIDENTIAL PARTY	R	R	D	D	D	D	R
DEMOCRATIC MAJORITY	54%	65%	60%	60%	68%	57%	56%
PERCENT OF ALL CONTROVERSIAL ROLL CALLS[a]							
Party Coalitions							
ND + SD	29	30	42	35	17	16	12
Bipartisan Coalitions							
SD + R	6	8	4	3	13	18	21
ND + R	6	7	7	3	1	3	1
No Coalitions[b]	60	55	47	59	69	63	66
(N)	136	137	159	140	223	253	184

[a] Percents may not sum to 100 because of rounding.
[b] Combines rows 2 and 3 from Table 8.1.

nant occurrence in the House. Distinguishing under what conditions coalitions will and will not form becomes one important follow-up question.

Importance and Decline

Table 8.2 shows the importance of Democratic Party coalition activity within this larger pattern. We can see the decline in Democratic Party coalitions over time and the corresponding increase in the bipartisan conservative coalition. As the table makes clear, in the years before the 89th Congress, the party coalition dominated coalition activity (compared to the other two possible coalitions) and both bipartisan coalitions occurred infrequently and at about the same rate. By the Johnson and Nixon years of the 90th and 91st congresses, the conservative coalition occurred most frequently, becoming the predominant coalition in the House. In fact, by the 91st Congress, the Democratic party coalition had approached the low frequency shown for both bipartisan coalitions in the earlier years. We have, then, one measure for the "importance" of party coalitions compared across time, and a measure of "decline." We find a change in Southern Democratic choice of partner from the Northern Democrats to Republicans and the corresponding change from party to bipartisan coalitions.[6]

---

[6] For further discussion of this realignment, see Barbara Sinclair, "Political Upheaval and Congressional Voting," *Journal of Politics* 38 (May 1976): 326–45.

It is also clear from Table 8.2 that these results bear no relation to such external partisan events as a change in the president's party or the size of the Democratic majority elected. Democratic Party coalitions were strong through a Republican and a Democratic presidential term and then dropped sharply during a Democratic and a Republican term. Congresses with the smallest Democratic majority (the 85th) and the second largest (the 86th) show virtually identical coalition outcomes, while congresses similar in Democratic size and Democratic presidents (87th, 88th, and 90th) show very different outcomes. The most one could say, cutting into the chronological pattern, is that in the years when coalitions were predominant (the 85th through 88th), they formed somewhat more frequently under same-party (Democratic) presidents than under other-party (Republican) presidents. Party coalitions were also slightly more frequent in the Democratic presidential 90th compared to the Republican presidential 91st.

The same kind of analysis can be applied across issues to see if the aggregate pattern is blurring more specific effects. Major issues are defined as those producing more than one controversial roll call (i.e., coalition situation) per congress for the seven congresses of the study, with all other issues combined into a miscellaneous category.[7] Outcomes are reported in Table 8.3 for the years of predominant party coalitions (85th–88th) and for the years of predominant conservative coalitions (90th, 91st). The 89th Congress represents a mixed and transitional case and is therefore omitted. The earlier congresses include two Democratic and one Republican presidency (Kennedy, Johnson, and Eisenhower); the later congresses one Democratic and one Republican presidency (Johnson and Nixon). Of the four possible outcomes, including three coalitions and one no-coalition outcome, the table reports the first and second most frequently occurring outcome.

The table shows clearly the pervasiveness of the change in coalition-activity issues and the extent of the breakdown of the Democratic Party coalition in the House. Comparing party coalitions against the other two coalitions, the party dominated in the earlier congresses in nine out of ten issue categories—all but civil rights. By the 90th and 91st, the party predominated in only three: fiscal policy, public works, and government operations—what some writers have called the "government management" category.[8] The conservative coalition, which dominated no issues in the earlier years, became the most frequent coalition by the 90th and 91st con-

---

[7] For details, see Hinckley, "Coalitions in Congress." Issue categories can be identified following the House's own classification of issues by committee. House standing committees for the 91st Congress, as reported in the *U.S. Congressional Directory*, formed the basis for the classification. A "procedural" roll call on a substantive issue is counted in the substantive-issue category. All controversial roll calls, with the exception of a few private bills, can be included in the categories. Note that the results closely reproduce those found in Clausen's *How Congressmen Decide*, with the present study adding House procedure, public works, and appropriations as three major issue areas.

[8] Clausen, *How Congressmen Decide*.

Table 8.3 House Coalition Activity by Issues: Most Frequently Occurring Outcomes[a]

ISSUE	85th–88th CONGRESSES (Party Coalitions Predominant)		90th–91st CONGRESSES (Conservative Coalitions Predominant)	
	1st	2nd	1st	2nd
Agriculture	ND + SD	no coalition	no coalition	SD + R
Fiscal	ND + SD	no coalition	no coalition	ND + SD
Public Works	ND + SD	no coalition	no coalition	ND + SD
House Procedure	ND + SD	no coalition	SD + R	no coalition
Civil Rights	ND + R	no coalition	no coalition	ND + R
Appropriations	no coalition	ND + SD	no coalition	SD + R
Foreign Affairs	no coalition	ND + SD	no coalition	SD + R
Domestic Welfare	no coalition	ND + SD	no coalition	SD + R
Govt. Operations	no coalition	ND + SD	no coalition	ND + SD
All Other Issues	no coalition	ND + SD	no coalition	SD + R

[a] The first and second most frequently occurring outcomes of the four possible coalition outcomes are reported in order of frequency.

gresses (six out of ten categories). The change in coalition activity extends across issues and is not merely an artifact of the aggregate pattern.

How "important," then, was the Democratic Party through the fourteen years of the study in organizing legislative resources to determine outcomes in the House? By this analysis, the Democratic Party was active in approximately 30–40 percent of these outcomes through the early years of the study, declining in importance to between 10 and 20 percent in the later congresses, the decline persistent and pervasive across issues.

Presidential Party and Party Coalition Activity

The second part of the inquiry can now be addressed. To what extent is party a "link" between the White House and House coalition activity? More specifically, is the presidency a resource in the sense that changes in partisan coalition activity are related to changes in the party or activity of the president? We will examine two major presidential conditions that could affect House coalition behavior. The first and most important to the immediate question is the president's party: whether there is same- or other-party control of the presidency in relation to the House. (With Democratic majorities in the House for all the years under study, same-party presidents are Democratic, other-party presidents are Republican.) The second condition is the activity of the president, measured by whether the president takes a stand on the roll call. This measure, of course, will not distinguish cases of intense presidential involvement from cases where someone in the liaison staff merely records the president's position. It will serve, however, to separate out the "purely" congressional activity from that of at least some presidential concern.

Following the presumption of party linkage, *activity by a president of the same party* could supply a resource directly—rallying partisans behind the presidential banner and, by reducing the costs of communication and increasing the expectation of rewards, making it easier for party coalitions to form. *Control of the White House by the same party* would operate in a broader, more diffused fashion. Providing greater access and executive information, posing less threat of presidential veto, it may also facilitate the forming of party coalitions more than under conditions of other-party control. Note that *activity by a president of either party* may affect coalition activity. This would indicate some presidential influence, but would not show any party effect.

Against these possibilities is the argument for independence developed for repetitive coalition games. The calculation of costs and expected returns over time makes the presidential resource less important. House coalition actors expect to outlast any eight-year presidential term. We should therefore expect little relationship between these presidential conditions and variations in House coalition activity.

It is important to understand the limits of the question being asked. It is not inquiring as to whether presidents affect legislation in any way or on any one bill of particular importance to them or whether they influence the votes of some individual members. Nor is it concerned with the many other ways a president may be a key participant in the legislative process. It inquires merely as to their effects on congressional coalition activity and specifically on party activity, measured by the tendency of party coalitions to dominate the organization of legislative resources compared to other coalitions.

COALITION ACTIVITY   Controlling for the chronological shift and realignment shown before, we can inquire about more marginal effects. See Table 8.4. Comparing first merely the incidence of party coalitions (ND + SD) versus all other coalition outcomes, the similarity across all presidential conditions is immediately apparent. Looking at the vertical comparisons, we can see that it is true that party coalitions are very slightly more frequent under conditions of same-party control. However, as the horizontal comparisons make clear, party coalitions are most frequent when presidents are inactive! No clear linkage with the president can be traced. Overall, by chi square results, *there is no significant difference* (1 df, two-tailed, for $p < .05$) *in the incidence of party coalition versus other forms of coalition activity according either to party control of the presidency or to presidential activity.* While the roll calls can be considered a sampling of an underlying continuum of con-

Table 8.4   House Coalition Activity: As Affected by Presidential Party and Presidential Activity

	PERCENT OF CONTROVERSIAL ROLL CALLS	
	Presidents Active	Presidents Inactive
SAME-PARTY PRESIDENTS (87th–90th)		
Party Coalitions	24	27
Bipartisan Coalitions	10	20
No Coalitions	66	53
(N)	(461)	(314)
OTHER-PARTY PRESIDENTS (85th, 86th, 91st)		
Party Coalitions	20	24
Bipartisan Coalitions	13	20
No Coalitions	67	56
(N)	(215)	(242)

gressional activity only in the very loosest sense, the statistic is helpful here in describing and emphasizing the important negative results. This is not an artifact of the particular party coalition chosen for analysis. Similar negative results can be seen with alternative definitions of party coalition activity.[9]

This same table supplies additional detail on presidential effects. Bipartisan coalitions (SD + R) are more likely to form when presidents are inactive; no-coalition results are more likely when presidents are active. The

[9] Alternative definitions of party coalitions can be examined against the same-versus-other-party presidential condition. Treating coalition players as *individual* House members, we can define party coalitions as a joining together of these members in sufficient numbers to assume this is not simply a chance combination. Following the 75 percent definition as above, a Democratic party coalition may be said to occur when at least 75 percent of the Democratic coalition players join together, and the same for Republicans. By this definition, Democratic Party coalitions are more likely to occur with same-party (Democratic) presidents, though the relationship is not perfectly consistent across the seven congresses. Republican Party coalitions, however, are also more likely to occur with Democratic Party presidents. In other words, since both coalitions form more frequently under Democratic than Republican presidents, the same versus other party condition does not affect House coalition activity.

Percent Party Coalitions of all Roll Calls

	R (85)	R (86)	D (87)	D (68)	D (89)	D (90)	R (91)
Democratic	46	62	74	76	71	49	36
Republican	49	63	60	71	61	53	42
N roll calls	(136)	(137)	(159)	(140)	(223)	(253)	(184)

results hold, it should be pointed out, for all four presidential administrations in the study. Chi square results show no significant difference (2 df. two-tailed, for p<.05) in the full distribution for the condition of presidential party control, but a significant difference ($\chi^2 = 25.5$, p <.01) for presidential activity.

It would appear, then, that the clearest difference in the table, remarkable otherwise for its lack of difference, is the decrease in coalition activity associated with presidential activity. Legislative coalitions, whether partisan or bipartisan, form more frequently when there is no presidential activity at all. Presidents may disrupt or inhibit congressional coalition activity, or it may be that the issues of greater interest to presidents are less amenable to successful coalition bargaining. In any case, this one effect does not support the party linkage notion. First, it works against rather than for the formation of coalitions. And second, it is associated with presidents of both parties. Moreover, in no case does party control of the White House affect the incidence of House coalition activity. This is the first important negative finding on the point.

COALITION SUCCESS   The effect for coalition activity is the same for coalition success, which is defined as being on the majority, or winning, side of the roll call. In triads where no one actor has sufficient resources to win alone, choice of partner can itself determine membership in the winning coalition. All congresses except the 89th show this condition. In the 89th, Northern Democrats were numerous enough to win at times even against the combined resources of Southern Democrats and Republicans. So there are a few instances in which a bipartisan coalition was active but did not win. There are no instances in which a partisan coalition was active but did not win. Therefore the activity rates for partisan coalitions in Table 8.4 are the same as their success rates. Party coalitions win from 20 to 27 percent of the time on controversial roll calls, whatever the presidential party or presidential activity. And there are no significant differences in party coalition success according to the various presidential conditions. This is the second important negative finding on the point.

COALITION ACTIVITY BY ISSUE   Presidents may affect coalition activity on some issues more than others, in which case the aggregate pattern would mask more specific issue effects. Two possibilities should be considered. First, presidents may influence the *kinds* of issues that will be raised at the controversial roll call stage: in other words, the raising of coalition situations. Agriculture or appropriations bills of the sort initiated by Republican presidents may not be initiated by Democratic presidents. Such issues might result in the same *rate* of coalition activity, but the absolute *number* of party or bipartisan coalitions would be different. For a second possibility, presidents may affect coalitions on some issues but not others. There may be no presidential effect on a large number of public works bills, but a sub-

Table 8.5 Presidential Condition and Frequency of Coalition Situation

SAME VERSUS OTHER PARTY CONTROL	PERCENT ROLL CALLS ON ISSUE OF ALL ROLL CALLS[a]										
	Domestic Welfare	Government Operations	Foreign Affairs	Appropriations	Public Works	All Other Issues	Fiscal	Agriculture	House Procedure	Civil Rights	Total All Roll Calls
Same Party	17	17	12	10	10	10	9	7	5	3	N = 775 (100%)
Other Party	17	16	12	14	12	11	4	7	3	3	N = 457 (99%)

[a] Based on all controversial roll calls. Percents may not sum to 100 due to rounding.

stantial effect on a smaller number of fiscal bills, the latter effect submerged in the overall pattern.

ISSUE FREQUENCY IN COALITION SITUATIONS   The first possibility can be answered clearly, and the answer is important. *There are nearly identical distributions of controversial roll calls* (or coalition situations) for Democratic and Republican administrations. (See Table 8.5.) There is a striking point-by-point matching of issue frequency. Domestic welfare bills comprise 17 percent of the coalition situations in Democratic administrations and 17 percent in Republican administrations, foreign affairs 12 percent in each administration, and so on down the line. The largest difference, in fact, is merely five percentage points, occurring on fiscal issues.[10]

So whatever the influence of the president at some earlier point in the legislative process, the results for frequency of controversial roll calls are the same. If we consider a controversial roll call to be a coalition situation, the presidential party does not affect the kind of coalition situation that is raised. Democratic administrations have been popularly linked with domestic welfare bills, Republican administrations with fiscal or agricultural affairs. Presidents themselves weight these differently—in their speeches,

[10] Across the four presidential administrations, the relative frequency of most issues remains the same. The exceptions are: foreign affairs, relatively more frequent in Kennedy and Nixon administrations; domestic welfare, relatively more frequent in the Eisenhower and Johnson administrations; and the miscellaneous "all other issues," increasing slightly in frequency in the two more recent (Johnson and Nixon) administrations. Note, however, that even these exceptions are associated with presidents of different parties.

Table 8.6 Presidents and Party Coalitions by Issue

	PERCENT DEMOCRATIC PARTY COALITIONS OF ALL ROLL CALLS ON THE ISSUE[a]								
	Agriculture	Fiscal	Public Works	Appropriations	All Other Issues	Government Operations	House Procedure	Foreign Affairs	Domestic Welfare
SAME VERSUS OTHER PARTY CONTROL									
Same Party Control	49	48	35	21	31	21	38	16	9
Other Party Control	30	—	53	27	28	21	—	8	8
SOME VERSUS NO ACTIVITY									
Presidents Active	43	44	41	22	24	18	—	17	8
Presidents Inactive	42	—	44	25	35	23	38	6	10

[a] No percentages are reported for N's of 25 or less. These cases are represented by a dash in the table. The civil rights issue, with virtually no party roll calls, is excluded. No issues showed significant differences ($p < .05$) in party coalition frequency for either same versus other party control or some versus no presidential activity: for chi square tests, 1 df, two-tailed.

personal efforts, and other setting of priorities. But by the roll call stage the frequency of issues raised is the same.

Within each category, of course, the definition of issues may change. A domestic welfare issue in one administration may change to another domestic welfare issue in another administration: a labor issue changes to education or to minimum wage. This would not be tapped in the present analysis. In terms of the present classification, however, no differences are apparent for White House party control. Measured merely at the roll call stage of coalition situations, presidential party does not affect the frequency of issues raised. This constitutes the third negative finding on the question.

The second possibility concerns the effect of presidential "partyness" on some issues more than others (see Table 8.6). The results support the earlier aggregate pattern. First, comparing conditions of presidential party control (the first two rows in the table), we find a slight increase in party coalitions under the same-party presidential condition in four of the seven issues compared. Agriculture issues appear to be the only fairly clear case of an association with White House control. Foreign affairs also shows some difference. Second, comparing presidential activity (the second two rows in the table), we find no increase in party coalitions under the active presidential condition. Indeed, party coalitions are at least as frequent or more frequent in almost all issues under conditions of presidential inactivity. The one exception is interesting: the foreign affairs area, traditionally considered an area of strongest presidential influence. It is the one issue in the table in which both party control and presidential activity are associated with an increase in party coalitions—where the notion of party "linkage" from the presidency receives some support. Nevertheless, it is also the issue marked by some of the lowest party activity overall. In chi square tests, *none of the issues showed significant differences* (for $p < .05$, 1 df, two-tailed) *in the tendency to form party coalitions for either of the presidential conditions*. The aggregate negative findings hold for the specific issue-by-issue effects. This is the fourth negative finding on the point.

In general, then, "partyness" in the White House has little effect on "partyness" in the House, measured by the tendency of party coalitions to dominate the organization of political resources. There is some slight increase in party coalition activity under conditions of same-party presidential control. However, party coalitions form most frequently when there is no presidential activity at all. And all differences reported are slight.

The picture that emerges is one of change in coalition partners, a decline in the importance of the Democratic Party coalition, and a pervasiveness of the change across issues. In the years when Democratic Party coalitions dominated the organization of legislative resources, they did so across a wide range of issues. The change to conservative coalition dominance was also pervasive across issues—both the pervasiveness and the change operating independently of presidential conditions. The one consistent presidential input into this generally impermeable situation works against party activity in the sense that it is associated with an increase in the no-coalition result. Presidents, then, may have one substantial input into legislative coalition behavior, but it is not attributable to their "partyness." First, it persists through all presidential-party situations, and second, it is inversely rather than positively related to the "partyness" of legislative coalition activity.

DISCUSSION

This chapter proposed that parties can be conceptualized within a coalition frame—thus brought outside of themselves—to permit comparative analysis and assessment. Viewed as one of a number of possible coalitions, they can be compared against others across time, across issues, or across varying political settings. We can examine the "decline" of parties, their "realignment," or their "importance" in one setting compared to others. Both parties and legislatures vary greatly across nations, but the chapter proposed that the relative frequency of party activity compared to other coalition activity can be measured and compared. Hence, we can compare party activity across legislatures, compare the durability of dominant coalitions, or compare the effects of elections, executive decisions, and other events.

Specifically, the argument was that repetitive as compared to single coalition games are relatively impermeable to external events. The resources and constraints imposed on the players from the ongoing coalition activity determine in large part the strategy and outcome of play, with any externally imposed resources and constraints correspondingly reduced in importance. To the extent that party coalitions operate in highly repetitive situations, we should expect less influence from such partisan phenomena as presidential or electoral conditions. Since parties operate in situations of varying degrees of repetitiveness, the proposition can be applied comparatively.

The argument was applied to House coalition behavior, the House offering an ideal test case of a highly repetitive coalition situation. Results show a change in coalition behavior over time and a pervasiveness across issues that are independent of various partisan external events. We find a breakdown of the Democratic Party coalition and emergence of a newly predominant conservative coalition extending across issues. Results further show, controlling for this chronological realignment, little effect on the incidence of party coalitions from presidential party control or activity. "Partyness" in the White House has little effect on "partyness" in the House, measured by the tendency of party coalitions to dominate the organization of political resources. There is a slight increase in party coalitions under conditions of same-party presidential control. However, party coalitions form most frequently when there is no presidential activity at all. Within this particular design, no linkage in the sense of a clear and positive relationship between presidential party and legislative party activity can be observed.

Congressional responsiveness to its own internal processes rather than external events is frequently deplored but less frequently explained. If this is the rational and expected coalition behavior in repetitive situations, the results point to the critical importance of membership turnover for reform. By changing the players' experience with the game and with the other players, altering the time perspective, and encouraging trust, increased turnover should produce very different coalition behavior and results. Following the argument that external influences should decrease in importance with the repetition of the situation, a change in turnover would change the responsiveness to external events.

The same inquiry could be applied to the Republican Party, to alternative definitions of the Democratic Party, or to comparative legislative designs. The hypothesis could be tested against legislatures that vary in the repetitive nature of their controversies, and against other arguments for congressional coalition formation.[11] This study of coalitions in one natural political setting can be added to other studies using other approaches.

Coalition analysis should offer a fruitful approach for the study of parties—in sharpening conceptualization, inviting comparisons, and in the number of specific inquiries which it could address. It can analyze parties within one system, it can compare them across systems, it can even return them from their isolated, special status to the larger political setting of which they are a part.

[11] See Barry Weingast, "A Rational Choice Perspective on Congressional Norms," *American Journal of Political Science* 23 (May 1979): 245–62; Kenneth Shepsle, "Institutional Arrangements and Equilibrium in Multidimensional Voting Models," *American Journal of Political Science* 23 (February 1979): 27–59; and David Koehler, "Legislative Coalition Formation: The Meaning of Minimal Winning Size with Uncertain Participation," *Midwest Journal of Political Science* 19 (1975): 27–39. Weingast argues that universalistic norms in legislatures can lead to larger-than-minimum coalitions and the tendency, at least in the short run, for pork-barrel politics. Shepsle shows how particular institutional arrangements in Congress help to explain coalition formation; and Koehler argues that the players' uncertainty about resources can lead to slightly larger-than-minimum coalitions, the players estimating how much, given uncertainty, should be necessary to ensure a minimum win.

Chapter 9

International Coalitions

The causes and effects of alliances between nations have received intensive political study. Writers have detailed the problems of building or maintaining a particular alliance and have examined the effects on an international system. Balance of power theories have predicted the consequences of alliance configurations in which no single state or alliance of states has a preponderant amount of power compared to others.[1] The formation, cohesion, impact, and dissolution of alliances have been studied.[2] Alliance formation has been examined at length as part of the "correlates of war."[3]

This literature has developed independently of coalition analysis and, like many other political subject matters, has its own distinct terminology and set of questions. Nevertheless, the combinatorial possibilities of the two approaches are obvious. The coalition framework should clarify and broaden the international inquiry, and the international behavior should add to the understanding of coalitions. What can be done for this one political sub-

---

[1] Morton Kaplan, *System and Process in International Politics* (New York: Wiley, 1957). For an analysis and review of this large body of literature, see Dina Zinnes, "An Analytical Study of the Balance of Power Theories," *Journal of Peace Research* 4 (1967): 270–88; and "Coalition Theories and the Balance of Power," in *The Study of Coalition Behavior*, ed. Sven Groennings et al. (New York: Holt, Rinehart and Winston, 1970), pp. 351–68.

[2] See George Liska, *Nations in Alliance* (Baltimore: Johns Hopkins Press, 1962).

[3] The Correlates of War Project was conducted at the University of Michigan by J. David Singer and associates. See Singer and Melvin Small, "Alliance Aggregation and the Onset of War, 1915–1945," in *Quantitative International Politics* (New York: Free Press, 1968) pp. 247–86, and "Formal Alliances, 1816–1965: An Extension of the Basic Data," *Journal of Peace Research* 6 (1969): 257–82. See also Singer et al., eds. *Explaining War* (Beverly Hills and London: Sage Publications, 1979) and a number of follow-up studies.

ject matter can be done for others. We can look, then, at this literature on alliances and see how it might be studied as a problem in coalition analysis.

CONCEPTUALIZATION

International alliances refer to the joining together of nations, usually on the basis of a written agreement, for mutual benefit of a military nature.[4] Purely economic alliances and other non-military agreements tend to be excluded in the usual discussions. Nations, or more precisely the particular individuals and organizations who govern their activities, constitute the basic unit of analysis. The activity of "nations" throughout this discussion implies the will and intelligence of their human governing agents. Nations, then, seek alliances to maximize benefits or minimize costs typically of a military nature. Alliances can be formed to deter aggression, counter another military threat, gain advantage of territory or other resources, or create a stable peace necessary for the pursuit of other activities. They are thus rational attempts on the part of these national units to preserve or promote their own self-interest.

It is clear that the alliances that have been studied so intensively are kinds of coalitions. They are formed between nations in an international mixed-motive situation; there are opportunities for conflict and coordination—in the sharing of waterways, aggression, political domination, war. In forming these coalitions, nations seek their own self-interest (or "national security") and attempt to gain "less than they might desire but more than they could achieve by acting alone."

The study of these alliances has a number of advantages for the student of coalitions. The actors are discrete autonomous units. Written agreements can often be used to identify when a coalition has occurred. The universe of potential actors can be identified—as that international "system" of nations that interact with each other and whose actions have implications for each other and for the system as a whole. In contrast to the legislative coalitions studied previously, we can more easily identify the situation, the players, and the game. There are advantages also in the range of approaches possible. The discrete units, assumption of rationality, and limited number of nations usually involved in a coalition situation are ideally suited for game theory. Indeed, many of the questions raised in the following section can be analyzed in game-theoretic terms. A number of international simulations exist and can be used for experimental designs. While international games pose unusually high stakes, the stakes of the game in the experiment can be

---

[4] See, for example, Bruce Bueno de Mesquita and J. David Singer, "Alliances, Capabilities, and War," in *Political Science Annual*, Vol. 4, ed. Cornelius Cotter (Indianapolis, Ind.: Bobbs-Merrill, 1973), p. 241.

Figure 9.1 Major-Power Alliances, 1900–1914

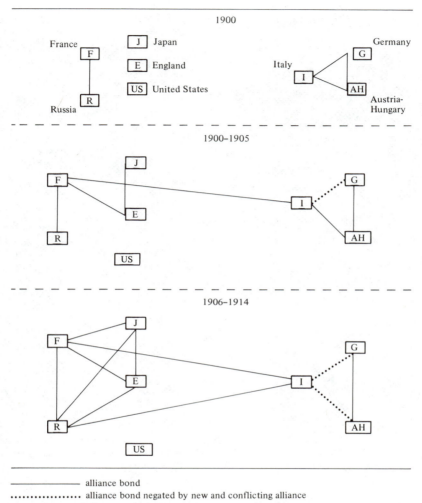

—————— alliance bond
················ alliance bond negated by new and conflicting alliance

Source: Alan Sabrosky, "From Bosnia to Sarajevo," in *Explaining War*, ed. J. David Singer (Beverly Hills and London: Sage Publications, 1979), p. 145. © 1979. Reprinted by permission of the publisher.

manipulated or controlled. Alliances also can be studied in natural political settings, and considerable effort has been spent in compiling data for this.

Thus we can analyze changes in coalition formation of the major-power subsystem of the period 1900–14, where the major powers are taken to be England, France, Russia, Germany, Austria-Hungary, Italy, the United States, and Japan.[5] The top third of Figure 9.1 shows the situation at the

[5] Alan Sabrosky, "From Bosnia to Sarajevo," in *Explaining War*, p. 145.

Figure 9.2   Alliance Configurations: A Two-Dimensional Illustration

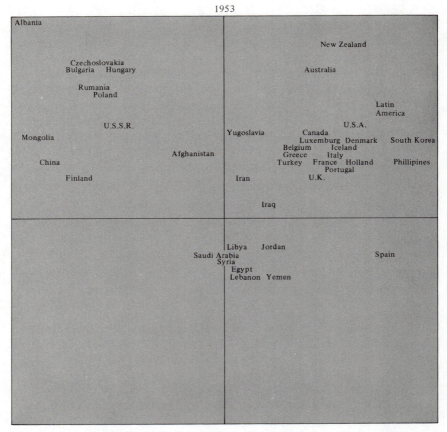

Source: Adapted from Michael Wallace, "Alliance Polarization, Cross-Cutting, and International War, 1815–1964," in *Explaining War*, ed. J. David Singer (Beverly Hills and London: Sage Publications, 1979), pp. 92, 93. © 1979. Reprinted by permission of the publisher.

turn of the century: the Franco-Russian coalition potentially opposed the coalition of Germany, Italy, and Austria-Hungary, with three nations not forming coalitions. By 1905, coalition activity had increased. England formed coalitions with France and Japan, and the Franco-Italian pact effectively broke the Italian-German coalition. A coalition actor, we said in Chapter 5, will tend not to be simultaneously in coalition with two opponents. The bottom third of the figure shows the situation immediately before the outbreak of World War I. Coalition activity had increased until it involved all of the major powers except the United States, while Italy had been separated from the Dual Alliance of Germany and Austria-Hungary. France, England, Russia, and Japan—all would enter war against Germany and Austria-Hungary within one month of each other in 1914.

Finland Czechoslovakia Bulgaria
Hungary
Rumania
East Germany
Poland

Mongolia

U.S.S.R.   Burma

                    Afghanistan
South Korea   China

Taiwan

                              Iran
        Phillipines
        Australia Pakistan
        Thailand   Iraq   Africa
                                    Saudi Arabia
        New Zealand Turkey   Libya
        France   U.K.
  U.S.A.   Holland
Latin   Denmark Belgium Greece   Syria Kuwait
America   Canada Luxemburg   Lebanon Yemen
        Iceland Italy West Germany   Jordan
            Portugal   Malagasy

                        Yugoslavia

            Malaysia

    Spain

Another, more quantitative, example of the kind of analysis possible was suggested by Michael Wallace. Wallace analyzed the nations in an international system to show the relative distance of each nation from the others in its alliance behavior.[6] In addition to formal alliances, Wallace considered memberships in the same international organizations and the existence of formal diplomatic relations. The closeness or distance of a pair of nations was measured not only by direct ties with each other, but also by the number of ties (i.e., the incidence of alliance behavior) that the pair shared with other nations. Thus nations A and B, each of whom has an alli-

[6] Michael Wallace, "Alliance Polarization, Cross-Cutting, and International War," in *Explaining War*, pp. 83–112. This is merely one of many alternative methods.

ance with C, are closer in the matrix than two other nations without such an additional alliance.

Figure 9.2 shows the alliance configurations resulting from this analysis for the years 1953 and 1963. Both years show the expected Cold War configuration of distinct American and Russian alliance patterns, with a third bloc of nations unaligned with the superpowers and in alliance with each other. Changes across the decade are also apparent. The United States moved more centrally into an alliance pattern whereas Russia became more separated. Some individual nations changed their positions dramatically. We can notice, in particular, China, South Korea, Yugoslavia, and Iraq.

For another example, recall the linked coalitions of Chapter 6. The diagrams shown in that chapter can be taken to represent an international system, with the double lines in the diagrams the alliances between nations. Many other ways of conceptualizing international coalition behavior could also be proposed.

RESEARCH QUESTIONS AND HYPOTHESES

A major preoccupation of international relations has been the study of war. Coalition activity is of interest primarily for its effect upon wars—their incidence, length, intensity, and payoffs to winners and losers. Wars, therefore, and the various war-related effects become the dependent variables in these studies, and the kinds of coalition activity become the independent variables.

Balance of power theories, using a number of different arguments, predict that a particular kind of alliance configuration will inhibit the occurrence of war. When nations are allied such that no one nation or alliance can dominate the others, a status quo will be maintained; no nation or alliance can aggress, or attempt other kinds of aggrandizement, without being blocked by the others. Each nation finds that it cannot improve its situation beyond the present distribution of returns. Change, indeed, threatens a worse outcome. Note that a number of different alliance formations meet the balance of power condition:[7]

- no alliances, with all states equal
- all states in alliances, with the alliances equal
- some states in alliances and some unaligned states, with the alliances equal to and not less than any one unaligned state.

[7] For a somewhat different analysis, see Zinnes, "Coalition Theories and the Balance of Power." An excellent game-theoretic analysis of the contribution of a "balancer" nation to international stability is provided by Philip Schrodt, "Richardson's N-Nation Model and the Balance of Power," *American Journal of Political Science* 22 (May 1978): 364–90.

The critical independent variable is the balance of resources shared by the various alliances—or put differently, the kind of coalition formation in which a balance of resources occurs. Nations in such a situation would restrict any activity that threatened this balance: for instance, a change in coalition partners, another nation's entry into or departure from the system, or the attempt by any nation to increase its resources at the expense of others. Peace may be less the intent than the by-product of this situation. Nevertheless, according to these theories, *coalition formation resulting in a balance of resources between the various coalitions reduces the likelihood of war.*

Other kinds of coalition activity lead to different results. According to some arguments, *alliance aggregation may increase the likelihood of war*, by locking nations into so many alliances that any one act of aggression quickly spreads throughout the system as a whole. The "entangling alliances" in Europe on the eve of the First World War would be cited as a case in point. Alliance aggregation has been measured by the number of separate alliances formed and the percentage of nations in an international system involved in alliances, as well as by other indicators. Preliminary investigation shows mixed results: in the nineteenth century, a negative relationship between alliance aggregation and war (the more aggregation the less chance of war) and in the twentieth century a positive relationship (the more aggregation the more chance).[8]

Alliance aggregation however, includes many different kinds of coalition activity, and each may have separate effects on the occurrence of war. In a preliminary study, Bruce Bueno de Mesquita examined six independent variables for their relationship with war.[9] They included

(1) the polarity of coalition activity: i.e., whether coalitions result in a bipolar (two-coalition) or multipolar (more than two-coalition) alignment of nations
(2) the "tightness" of coalition activity: i.e., the extent, or amount, of coalition activity within one alignment
(3) the "discreteness" of coalition activity: i.e., the extent, or amount, of coalition activity across separate alignments
(4) a change in polarity
(5) a change in tightness
(6) a change in discreteness.

We can observe that some of the variables refer to the kind of coalition formed, some to the amount of coalition formation, as well as the kind, and some to the stability of coalitions. *The polarity, the tightness, or the discreteness of coalition activity may affect the occurrence of war; or changes in any of these three may affect its occurrence.* Nations, Bueno de Mesquita hypothesized, may be prompted into war as a result of the uncertainty produced by the

---

[8] Singer and Small, "Alliance Aggregation and the Onset of War."
[9] Bruce Bueno de Mesquita, "Systemic Polarization and the Occurrence and Duration of War," in *Explaining War*, pp. 113–38.

change in alliance. His results suggest that the change in coalition activity is, indeed, more important than its polarity, tightness, or discreteness.

The nature of the alliance affects not only the occurrence of war, but the distribution of spoils when the war is over. In one study explicitly concerned with coalitions, Harvey Starr examined *how the "payoffs of war" are influenced by the attributes of the war coalition.*[10] He sought to explain the distribution of payoffs by different models of coalition activity: those emphasizing the initial distribution of resources nations bring to the coalition; those emphasizing the likeness, in ideology or community, of the coalition partners; and those emphasizing the extent of their participation and commitment in the war. Twenty-one hypotheses were developed and tested with a variety of measures. Overall, Starr found that all three kinds of variables are important to the results, although the participation and commitment variable shows the largest influence.

Dependent variables beyond war are addressed in some of the alliance studies. *Factors affecting the durability of alliances* (i.e., the stability of coalitions) have been given attention. The number of nations in an alliance, their degree of commitment, change in resources, and the number of major powers in an alliance can all affect durability.[11] *Factors affecting the redistribution of resources among alliance participants* have also been studied, beyond the payoffs of war.[12] The balance of power theories, in fact, make direct predictions about durability and about redistribution of resources. In many of the formulations, peace is merely the byproduct: the direct result of the balance is to continue the resource distribution and the alliances of the status quo. The results might be diagramed:

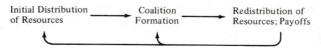

A particular kind of coalition produces results that reinforce the stability of the coalition and reproduce the original resource distribution, leading the coalition situation to perpetuate itself.

Extending the Research Questions

This research can be extended from the study of coalitions. The international literature treats coalition formation as the independent variable—as a

[10] Harvey Starr, *War Coalitions: The Distribution of Payoffs and Losses* (Lexington, Mass.: D. C. Heath, 1972).

[11] For summary and review of this literature, see Bueno de Mesquita and Singer, "Alliances, Capabilities, and War," pp. 263–68.

[12] Ibid., pp. 253–63; see also Mancur Olson, Jr. and Richard Zeckhauser, "An Economic Theory of Alliances," in *Economic Theories of International Politics*, ed. Bruce Russett (Chicago:

critical influence on other results; and it examines the alliance configuration of the international system as a whole. It asks, for example, how the polarity or the balance of power between coalitions already formed affects other international behavior. But what factors produce a change in discreteness or tightness or polarity—or a change from bipolarity to multipolarity? If these configurations are important, we need to ask how they are produced: what, in other words, affects the forming of coalitions between individual nations? An alliance configuration is merely an aggregate product of such inter-nation decisions. It is the individual nations, we assume, that decide to make or break alliances, go to war, or bargain with other nations to preserve the peace.

What, indeed, is the extent of individual nations' coalition activites in an international system of linked coalitions? We can extend analysis to the points raised in Chapter 6. What is the range of options confronting a nation in forming alliances—in empirical practice and in game-theory prescriptions? To what extent are these decisions constrained by other past and present alliances? The proposition was advanced previously that an actor in more than one coalition situation would not be simultaneously in coalition and opposition with another actor. The international studies could tell us the empirical frequency of such an occurrence.

Repetitive games introduce constraints not found in a single play of the game: some variables are reduced and some increased in importance. If international alliance formation is similar in repetition to congressional coalition behavior, the same calculus of choice may underlie the two superficially dissimilar situations. Chapter 5 proposed that stable alliances can determine the range and kind of conflict possible for all actors—prohibiting conflict in one sphere that would threaten the trust between traditional partners in another sphere. A change in a traditional alignment would produce a corresponding change in the kinds of issues producing conflict. The "trouble spots" in one area would appear or disappear because of the coalitions formed in another area. The preceding chapter showed one instance of this behavior for coalitions in Congress. The same effect should be examined for international alliances.

The international studies have counted the cases in which alliances form, but the nonevents—the cases in which no alliances form—need counting as well. The decision not to form a coalition is itself worth study, both for its causes and effects. It would also produce a very different picture of alliance configurations. Nonevents, of course, are notoriously difficult to observe. Nevertheless, defining a set of international decisions, as we de-

---

Markham, 1968), pp. 25–45. Olson and Zeckhauser developed a model analyzing nations' initial resources and contributions to a coalition. The model, supported by data from the NATO alliance, explains why major powers contribute relatively more, compared to other nations, to a coalition. See also Francis Beer, *The Political Economy of Alliances*, (Beverly Hills and London: Sage Publications, 1972).

Fig. 9.3   Coalition Research and International Alliances: The Two Literatures Combined[a]

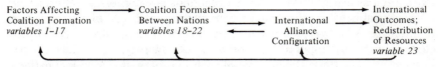

[a]Variable numbers refer to the numbers given in Table 4.1.

fined a set of congressional decisions, may be a feasible research undertaking. The relative frequency of no-coalition and coalition outcomes could then be measured and compared for various conditions.

Within an individual nation's range of choices, how important are the variables previously identified in this study? How do they affect the initial choice of partner, the decision to join or not to join a coalition, and the particular coalition formed? What is the relative importance of a nation's initial resource distribution compared to its historical friendships and animosities, and compared to its ideological likeness to other nations? Coalition analysis can accumulate information from diverse approaches and subject areas. It can address the effects of information on choice of partner and the conditions under which frontrunners (or major powers or aggressors) are blocked or supported. International studies could benefit from and contribute to finding the answers to these questions.

The diagram in Figure 9.3 shows the two kinds of studies in combination; the arrows respresent the potential research questions. The international literature has focused primarily on the right-hand portion of the diagram. The coalition studies from the left-hand portion could profitably be added to that analysis.

VARIABLES AND MEASURES

It is clear from the foregoing review that the study of alliances is still in its early stages. Many of the predictive variables have not been fully identified or distinguished from each other. The concept of alliance aggregation is thought to be important, but all the many ways alliances can be aggregated remain to be distinguished. Aggregation in terms of the kinds of coalitions formed needs to be separated from aggregation as amount, or extent, of coalition activity. Alliance aggregation is predicted to increase the chance of war, and a balance of power to decrease the chance; hence, all those aggregated alliances that are also balances of power need to be excluded before the predictions can be tested. We face the kind of complex problem for which a combination of approaches should be particularly useful. Game theory and experimental simulations, for instance, can isolate factors that are not easily separated in the actual international events. At the same time, a more systematic study of the events themselves can be undertaken.

Nevertheless, we should recognize that many of the factors identified as important to alliances can now be operationalized and measured. Moreover, they are familiar from earlier chapters as important to students of coalitions. Listing the coalition variables (with reference to the numbers in Table 4.1), we can see how they can be measured with the international data. The measures being reported are drawn from the Correlates of War Project, conducted by J. David Singer and associates at the University of Michigan. This is not meant to exclude or deemphasize other work or other kinds of approaches, but merely to illustrate the kind of measurement now available.

Initial Resource Distribution: Power Rankings (Variables 6 and 8)

Theodore Caplow distinguished types of coalition situations by the relative power among the actors, merely specifying which actor has more or less power than others. Students of alliances also use power rankings: typically, a distinction between the "major powers" and all other nations. Balance of power theories require at least this same relative ranking. We in fact have available a list of major powers for specific time periods. For example, before World War I, the major powers are identified as shown in Figure 9.1. After the Second World War they include the United States, Russia, Britain, France, and Communist China.[13] Other historical accounts could also supply these power rankings. Therefore, the kind of analysis Caplow and others have conducted can be carried out with data from these international studies.

Initial Resource Distribution: Other Measures of Resources (Variables 6 and 8)

In some studies in which payoffs are calculated and choice of partner predicted from the initial resource distribution, a quantitative measurement of resources is desirable. These measures, too, are available for nations. Harvey Starr worked with two measures in his study of war coalitions. One combined indicators of a nation's major power status, population, diplomatic status, and military power. The other was derived from military and industrial capacity.[14] Another study used the "percentage share" of the total resources available to the major powers at a given time. The resources were calculated and combined into a single measure based on six separate indica-

---

[13] Singer and Small, "Formal Alliances, 1816–1965," p. 259.
[14] Starr, *War Coalitions*, esp. pp. 46, 47.

Table 9.1   Distribution of Major-Power Resources, 1900–1913

STATE	PERCENTAGE SHARE OF RESOURCES			
	1900	1905	1910	1913
France	10.1	9.8	9.6	10.4
Russia	16.1	16.5	16.5	16.7
England	20.6	16.5	15.0	14.1
Germany	16.7	16.9	17.2	18.2
Austria-Hungary	6.1	6.2	6.4	6.1
Italy	4.9	5.0	4.9	5.0
Japan	3.8	4.3	4.5	4.4
United States	21.6	24.9	25.9	25.0

Source: Alan Sabrosky, "From Bosnia to Sarajevo," in *Explaining War*, ed. J. David Singer. (Beverly Hills and London: Sage Publications, 1979), p. 146. Compiled from data available at The Correlates of War Project, University of Michigan. ©1979. Reprinted by permission of the publisher.

tors: total population, urban population, energy consumption, iron/steel production, military expenditures, and military personnel.[15] An illustration of this measure is shown for the European major powers before the First World War (see Table 9.1). Note the almost perfect mathematical balance of resources in 1900 between the France-Russian coalition and the coalition of Germany, Austria-Hungary, and Italy. Judging by the results, however, the 1900 balance was not stable. With changes in resource distribution and the forming of the Anglo-French coalition, that balance was upset.

Any measurement of power is the subject of extensive debate, and national power measures are no exception. Nevertheless, if used with appropriate caution, these and other indicators of a nation's resource distribution are available for studying coalition behavior.

Policy or Ideological Distance: "Likeness" (Variable 5)

The likeness among actors—in policy, ideology, or cultural background—can override initial resources, affecting bargaining, choice of partner, and final coalition formed. A number of indicators are available to measure this likeness between nations. They can be used separately or combined into various composite measures. Starr developed an "Ideology/Community

[15] See Sabrosky, "From Bosnia to Sarajevo," pp. 144–46.

Score" based on the following indicators, among others, to measure likeness between any two nations A and B:

- reciprocal trade
- a common frontier
- racial similarity
- similarity in the dominant language
- similarity in the dominant religion
- similarity of governmental or constitutional system
- similarity of the degree of personal liberty in the nation
- scale of agreement on the ideological position of the two nations.[16]

Agreement should be possible among researchers, at least when scoring the first six indicators on the list—although weighting these components for any overall index looks difficult.

Past Experience with the Other Players (Variable 4)

Other indicators used in the Ideology/Community Score describe the past experience of coalition actors. Past experience, as we have seen throughout the earlier chapters, can be a critical influence on present coalition formation. So for nations A and B, we ask the following questions:

- Were A and B enemies or allies in the last war both engaged in?
- For a given time period, do the number of months of being allies exceed the number of months of being enemies?
- Were there any treaties or other agreements between A and B before the war in question?
- How would one classify the type of treaty (i.e., the extent of commitment between A and B)?
- Were there any other traditional rivalries between the two nations?
- Were there any other recent rivalries?
- Were any treaties broken by A or B with each other?
- Were any other diplomatic affronts or humiliations committed?
- Has there been any personal antagonism between the rulers of A and B?

Overlapping Membership (Variable 7)

Independently of likeness and past experience, overlapping membership in separate coalitions can influence the choice of coalition partner. In a system of linked coalitions (linked by overlapping membership), coalition behavior

---

[16] Starr, War Coalitions, p. 45. Altogether, seventeen indicators were used for the score. They are separated here into coalition variables 4 and 5.

Table 9.2 Winning Coalitions and the Distribution of Returns from War

WAR	NUMBER OF NATIONS IN WINNING COALITION	NUMBER OF MAJOR POWERS IN WINNING COALITION	NUMBER OF NATIONS RECEIVING SPOILS[a]	INDEX OF EQUITY[b] Territory	Indemnity
Crimean (1853–56)	5	4	1	80.00	—
Austro-Prussian (1866)	2	2	2	22.34	50.00
Franco-Prussian (1870–71)	4	1	4	0.00	0.00
Boxer Rebellion (1900)	11	8	11	—	52.61
First Balkan (1912–13)	4	0	4	44.81	—
Second Balkan (1913)	5	0	5	35.77	—
World War I (1914–18)	11	6	10	85.57	—
World War II (1939–45)	21	4	15	82.81	90.29

[a] Territory or indemnity.

[b] The index of equity ranges from 0 to 100, with 0 representing perfect equity between the nations. Thus, the higher the number, the greater the inequity in distribution of spoils. A dash indicates that data were not available.

Source: Adapted from data in Harvey Starr, *War Coalitions* (Lexington, Mass.: Lexington Books, 1972). See pp. 5, 39–41, and Appendixes A and E.

at any one point affects and is affected by coalitions formed elsewhere. Identifying the alliances among nations for any given time period automatically supplies this measure of overlapping membership.

Coalition Results (Variables 18–23)

All of the coalition results identified as dependent variables in Chapter 4 could be measured with the alliance data. Simply identifying the alliances in an international system, with the dates of their formation and ending, allows us to measure the choice of partner (18), whether or not a coalition forms (19), and the stability of the coalition over time (20). Adding relative power rankings provides a measure for the tendency to form revolutionary or conservative coalitions (21) and for whether or not the initially strongest player is included in a winning coalition (22). Adding the resource distributions among nations at different time points provides a measure of the returns or payoffs from the coalition (23). For example, we could calculate for the nations shown in Table 9.1 the payoffs at different time points from their respective coalitions. Other kinds of payoffs could also be specified—as, for example, winning or losing wars or other returns from war coalitions.

An illustration of such a payoff distribution is shown in Table 9.2. The table shows, for selected wars across a century's time, the distribution of territory and indemnity for the winning coalition members.[17] (Indemnity is payment of material goods, such as money or other physically transferable things.) An equity index from 0 to 100 measures the distribution of territory and indemnity to winning coalition members: the higher the index, the less equity in the distribution of returns. A perfect index score of 0 means that each member of the winning coalition received its mathematically average share (e.g., four members would each receive 25 percent of the returns). As the table makes clear, considerable inequity has existed in payment from war coalitions. We can therefore ask what factors relating to the coalition actors (the individual nations), the process, or the kind of coalition formed can explain these differences in returns. Other, less material payoffs can also be calculated: for example improvements in political or economic influence; the installation of more-friendly governments or other security; and the satisfaction of revenge, nationalistic drives, or cultural goals.

The point should be clear from the above illustration. A data set on international alliances is available for the study of coalitions. Even from the measures now available, we can investigate a number of central questions—asking who joins with whom, under what conditions, and with what effects for individual nations and the larger international system. So while coalition analysis can extend the study of alliances, the international data can also add greatly to research on coalitions.

---

[17] Ibid., esp. pp. 39–41 and appendixes.

Chapter 10

Summary

We have come far in this study through territory familiar and unfamiliar, and have marked out specific lines of inquiry and a larger area to be explored. No "conclusion" is appropriate to such a continuing venture, but we should, by way of summary, try to consolidate the progress achieved.

The book's major theme is that the study of coalitions can be broadly applied to the study of politics. A definition of coalition activity supplies a definition of politics as well. Coalition activity, as traditionally defined, includes three necessary components: a collective activity; a combination of conflict and coordination; and an exercise of power. These three in combination seem peculiarly essential to political action, the collective mixed-motive situation being precisely the kind of human problem that requires political skills. Resources have to be joined, power exercised, and outcomes determined in a situation in which people, forced to occupy a planet together, clash too much to form a team and coincide too much to go to war. In a political situation, one is engaged in collective activity, concerned with an exercise of power (defined broadly as using resources to determine outcomes), and required to deal in some way with the combined conflict and coordination. Eliminate any of these components and one is engaged in some other nonpolitical human affair.

Broad claims for studying coalitions have been made before, attracting only a limited number of practitioners and yielding fairly meager results. Coalition research, according to one critic, was "originally hailed as a field of great promise [that] would enable us to put politics back into the political equation."[1] It has progressed, however, he continued, only by remaining theoretically "pure" of political complexity and contamination. He was speaking of the game-theoretic studies. So to "put politics back" in the field that originally promised to put politics back into the political equation, we need to extend both the scope and the method of our application. This is the second major theme of the book.

Students of politics have a range of approaches available in studying coalitions. There is no one typical mode or limiting technique. Many people have considered coalition theory to be synonymous with game theory, but we should now see that that is not the case. Much of game theory has concentrated on noncoalitional two-person games while some coalition theory has developed from social-psychological research. Altogether, there are three major approaches for studying coalitions, each with its own potential, cautions to be observed, and characteristic techniques. One may dislike mathematics, experiments, case studies, or roll calls, and still do coalition research.

As we extend the method, so we extend the scope of the inquiry—to a list of variables requiring political application, and to extensions in time and political space. Political actors are constrained by past alliances, the chance of future success, or perceptions that the game will or will not be repeated over time. They work within a larger political environment—of overlapping members and linked situations—where decisions at one point set in motion other decisions all the way down the line. Politics is more complex than poker or Parcheesi, and coalition analysis can be used to deal with this complexity. We can study the range and variety of effects of trust in politics or analyze behavior in repetitive games, linked coalitions, or boundary situations.

Admittedly provisional, this point of view is a promising one. It offers a conceptual base point, a way of looking at politics as a distinctive activity. It offers a framework for accumulating, organizing, and generalizing results. Thus, diverse approaches in different subject areas can be used in conjunction to develop some empirical theory. Experiments, game-theoretic formulations, and studies of very diverse natural political settings can all contribute to the "research schedule" set forth in Chapter 4. Finally, this viewpoint offers a way of distinguishing like and unlike things—of identifying common patterns within superficially diverse forms. Very different forms of government or kinds of political situations should show similar patterns of coalition behavior. These include conditions facilitating stable alliances, revolutionary coalitions, or bandwagons; the effects of information on choice of coalition partner; and the effects of overlapping membership on the kinds of boundary coalitions that are formed.

While this viewpoint supplies a new way of looking at politics, it supplies a new view of coalitions as well. We are not limited to notions of strat-

[1] Scott Flanagan, "Models and Methods of Analysis," in *Crisis, Choice, and Change*, ed. Gabriel Almond et al. (Boston: Little, Brown, 1973), p. 67.

egy or payoffs, or a view of coalitions that seems to glorify the seedier side of political life. The view is broadened by the political perspective to include any goals, any outcomes, any means of combining resources. The goals of coalition actors in political conventions include not only the "jobs" awarded in the experimental design or the payoffs calculated mathematically. They include policy satisfaction, ideological principles, and beliefs about leadership. Goals span the human range from world view to narrowest self-interest. Outcomes include an arms limitation agreement or a cotton subsidy, a new dictatorship or a cabinet post. Resources can be applied with vision and altruism as well as in sessions in smoke-filled rooms. Planet-sharing is difficult and sometimes dirty, but it should exhibit the range as well as the central tendency of its inhabitants. As Marianne Moore observed about poetry, "I, too, dislike it," but

> one discovers in
> it, after all, a place for the genuine.

Coalitions, too, can show political scientists something that is essential and genuine to the subject they study.

Bibliography

The bibliography is organized in terms of the major approaches to the study of coalitions, as set forth in Chapter 2. Part I cites the social-psychological literature and Part II the game-theoretic studies. Parts III and IV, comprising the empirical political work, are distinguished by major research emphasis: those studies dealing primarily with minimum winning coalitions (Part III) and all other studies (Part IV). Part V lists collections of separate studies. We can thus see at a glance the state of the field and the kind of advances possible.

There are difficulties with any classification of this kind. Some writers span two fields and some studies span two or more approaches. Articles concerned primarily with minimum winning coalitions raise other politically interesting questions. Nevertheless, the advantages of the classification in showing the state of research should outweigh the few individual distortions. The general decision rules are as follows. The social-psychological and political studies are classified by the discipline (academic department) of the author, even in those cases where social psychologists address a central political subject, as in the study of presidential nominations. Game-theoretic and empirical political studies are distinguished by their major contribution: those using game theory and citing empirical cases only as illustrations are put in the former category, and those combining game theory with a substantial empirical study are put in the latter category. In keeping with the discussion in Chapter 2, those studies using "coalition" loosely to mean merely collection or aggregation, as in the phrase "New Deal Coalition" or "electoral coalitions," are excluded. Game-theoretic studies of two-person games are also excluded.

The listings for Parts I and II are highly selective, including only major works or those directly of interest to students of politics. The listings from the much smaller literature of empirical political studies (Parts III and IV) are less selective. They include all books and articles in major professional journals that could be identified for the past two decades of research.

I Social-Psychological Coalition Research

Anderson, R. "Status Structures in Coalition Bargaining Games." *Sociometry* 30 (December 1967): 393–403.

Bonacich, P., et al. "Cooperation and Group Size in the N-Person Prisoner's Dilemma." *Journal of Conflict Resolution* 20 (December 1976): 687–706.

Bond, J., and W. E. Vinacke. "Coalitions in Mixed-Sex Triads." *Sociometry* 24 (March 1961): 61–75.

Burhans, D., Jr. "Coalition Game Research: A Reexamination." *American Journal of Sociology* 79 (September 1973): 389–408.

Caplow, T. "A Theory of Coalitions in the Triad." *American Sociological Review* 21 (August 1956): 489–93.

———. "Further Development of a Theory of Coalitions in the Triad." *American Journal of Sociology* 64 (March 1959): 488–93.

———. *Two Against One: Coalitions in Triads.* Englewood Cliffs, N.J.: Prentice-Hall, 1968.

Chaney, M. V., and W. E. Vinacke. "Achievement and Nurturance in Triads Varying in Power Distribution." *Journal of Abnormal Social Psychology* 60 (March 1960): 175–81.

Chertkoff, J. "The Effects of Probability of Future Success on Coalition Formation." *Journal of Experimental Social Psychology* 2 (July 1966): 265–77.

———. "A Revision of Caplow's Coalition Theory." *Journal of Experimental Social Psychology* 32 (1967): 172–77.

———. "Coalition Formation as a Function of Differences in Resources." *Journal of Conflict Resolution* 15 (September 1971): 371–83.

———. "Sociopsychological Views on Sequential Effects in Coalition Formation." *American Behavioral Scientist* 18 (March/April 1975): 451–71.

——— and J. Braden. "Effects of Experience and Bargaining Restrictions on Coalition Formation." *Journal of Personality and Social Psychology* 30 (July 1974): 169–77.

Cole, S. "Coalition Preference as a Function of Vote Commitment in Some Dictatorial 'Political Convention' Situations." *Behavioral Science* 16 (September 1971): 436–41.

Collins, B., and B. Raven. "Group Structure: Attraction, Coalitions, Communication and Power." In *Handbook of Social Psychology,* edited by G. Lindzey and E. Aronson, ch. 4, pp. 102–204; see especially pp. 127–37. Reading, Mass.: Addison-Wesley, 1969.

Coser, L., ed. *George Simmel*. Englewood Cliffs, N.J.: Prentice-Hall, 1965.

Emerson, R. "Power-Dependence Relations: Two Experiments." *Sociometry* 27 (September 1964): 282–93.

Festinger, L. "A Theory of Social Comparison Processes." *Human Relations* 7 (May 1954): 117–40.

Fox, J., and M. Guyer. " 'Public' Choice and Cooperation in N-Person Prisoner's Dilemma." *Journal of Conflict Resolution* 22 (September 1978): 469–81.

Friend, K. et al. "Bargaining Processes and Coalition Outcomes: An Integration." *Journal of Conflict Resolution* 21 (June 1977): 267–98.

Gamson, W. "A Theory of Coalition Formation." *American Sociological Review* 26 (June 1961): 373–82.

———. "An Experimental Test of a Theory of Coalition Formation." *American Sociological Review* 26 (August 1961): 565–73.

———. "Coalition Formation at Presidential Nominating Conventions." *American Journal of Sociology* 68 (September 1962): 157–71.

———. "Experimental Studies of Coalition Formation." In *Advances in Experimental Social Psychology*, edited by L. Berkowitz, ch. 1, pp. 81–110. New York: Academic Press, 1964.

Hoffman, P., L. Festinger, and D. Lawrence. "Tendencies toward Group Comparability in Competitive Bargaining." *Human Relations* 7 (May 1954): 141–59.

Homans, G. *Social Behavior: Its Elementary Forms*. New York: Harcourt Brace Jovanovich, 1961; rev. ed., 1974.

Kelley, H., and A. Arrowood. "Coalitions in the Triad: Critique and Experiment." *Sociometry* 23 (September 1960): 231–44.

Komorita, A., and J. Chertkoff. "A Bargaining Theory of Coalition Formation." *Psychological Review* 80 (May 1973): 149–62.

Komorita, A., and D. Meek. "Generality and Validity of Some Theories of Coalition Formation." *Journal of Personality and Social Psychology* 36 (April 1978): 392–404.

Komorita, A., and D. Dravitz. "Effects of Alternatives on Bargaining." *Journal of Experimental Social Psychology* 15 (March 1979): 147–57.

Laing, J., and R. Morrison. "Coalitions and Payoffs in Three Person Sequential Games: Initial Tests of Two Formal Models." *Journal of Mathematical Sociology* 3, no. 1 (1973): 3–25.

———. "Sequential Games of Status." *Behavioral Science* 19 (1974): 177–97.

Lieberman, B. "Experimental Studies of Conflict in Some Two-Person and Three-Person Games." In *Mathematical Methods in Small Group Processes*, edited by J. Criswell, H. Solomon, and P. Suppes, pp. 203–20. Stanford, Calif.: Stanford University Press, 1962.

———. "*i*-Trust: A Notion of Trust in Three-Person Games and International Affairs." *Journal of Conflict Resolution* 8 (September 1964): 271–80.

———. "The Sino-Soviet Pair: Coalition Behavior from 1921 to 1965." In

Sino-Soviet Relations and Arms Control, edited by M. Halperin, pp. 305–27. Cambridge, Mass.: M.I.T. Press, 1967.

———. "Coalition Formation and Change." In *Social Choice,* edited by B. Lieberman, pp. 83–114. New York: Gordon and Breach Science Publishers, 1971.

———. "Coalitions and Conflict Resolution." *American Behavioral Scientist* 18 (March/April 1975): 557–81.

Michener, H. A., and E. J. Lawler. "Revolutionary Coalition Strength and Collective Failure as Determinants of Status Reallocation." *Journal of Experimental Social Psychology* 7 (July 1971): 448–60.

Michener, H. A., and M. Lyons. "Perceived Support and Upward Mobility as Determinants of Revolutionary Coalition Behavior." *Journal of Experimental Social Psychology* 8 (March 1972): 180–95.

Murnighan, J., et al. "Coalition Formation in Tetrads: A Critical Test of Four Theories." *Journal of Psychology* 103 (November 1979): 209–19.

Ofshe, L., and R. Ofshe. *Utility and Choice in Social Interaction.* Englewood Cliffs, N.J.: Prentice-Hall, 1970.

Phillips, J., and L. Nitz. "Social Contacts in a Three-Person 'Political Convention' Situation." *Journal of Conflict Resolution* 12 (June 1968): 206–14.

Rapoport, A. "Prospects for Experimental Games." *Journal of Conflict Resolution* 12 (December 1968): 461–70.

Simmel, G. "The Number of Members as Determining the Social Form of the Group." *American Journal of Sociology* 8 (July 1902): 1–46, 158–96.

———. *The Sociology of George Simmel.* Translated and edited by K. Wolff. New York: Glencoe Press, 1950.

Stryker, S. "Coalition Behavior." In *Experimental Social Psychology,* edited by C. McClintock, pp. 338–80. New York: Holt, Rinehart and Winston, 1972.

Thibaut, J., and H. Kelley. *The Social Psychology of Groups.* New York: John Wiley, 1959.

Vinacke, W. E. "The Effects of Cumulative Score on Coalition Formation in Triads with Various Patterns of Internal Power." *American Psychologist* 14 (July 1959): 381.

——— and A. Arkoff. "Experimental Study of Coalitions in the Triad." *American Sociological Review* 22 (August 1957): 406–15.

Vinacke, W. E., D. Crowell, D. Dien, and V. Young. "The Effect of Information about Strategy on a Three-Person Game." *Behavioral Science* 11 (May 1966): 180–89.

Wahba, M. "Coalition Formation under Conditions of Uncertainty." *Journal of Social Psychology* 88 (October 1972): 43–54.

Webster, M., Jr., and L. Smith. "Justice and Revolutionary Coalitions: A Test of Two Theories." *American Journal of Sociology* 84 (September 1978): 267–92.

Willis, R. H. "Coalitions in the Tetrad." *Sociometry* 25 (December 1962): 358–76.

II Game-Theoretic Studies of Coalitions

Axelrod, R. *Conflict of Interest: A Theory of Divergent Goals with Applications to Politics.* Chicago: Markham, 1970.

Berl, J. E., R. McKelvey, P. Ordeshook, and M. Winer. "An Experimental Test of the Core in a Simple N-Person Cooperative Nonsidepayment Game." *Journal of Conflict Resolution* 20 (September 1976): 453–80.

Brams, S. "A Cost/Benefit Analysis of Coalition Formation in Voting Bodies." In *Probability Models of Collective Decision Making*, edited by R. Niemi and H. Weisberg. Columbus, Ohio: Charles Merrill, 1972.

———. *Game Theory and Politics.* New York: Free Press, 1975.

———. *The Presidential Election Game.* New Haven, Conn.: Yale University Press, 1978.

——— and J. Garriga-Pico. "Bandwagons in Coalition Formation." *American Behavioral Scientist* 18 (March/April 1975): 472–96.

Brams, S., and J. Heilman. "When to Join a Coalition, and with How Many Others, Depends on What You Expect the Outcome to Be." *Public Choice* 17 (Spring 1974): 11–26.

Brams, S., and W. Riker. "Models of Coalition Formation in Voting Bodies." In *Mathematical Application in Political Science*, edited by J. Herndon, ch. 4. Charlottesville, Va.: University of Virginia Press, 1972.

Browne, E., and P. Rice. "A Bargaining Theory of Coalition Formation." *British Journal of Political Science* 9 (January 1979): 67–87.

Bueno de Mesquita, B., and R. Niemi. "A Dynamic Theory of Coalition Formation." Paper delivered at Midwest Political Science Association Meeting, Chicago, April 1980.

Davis, M. *Game Theory: A Nontechnical Introduction.* New York: Basic Books, 1970.

DeSwaan, A. "An Empirical Model of Coalition Formation as an N-Person Game of Policy Distance Minimization." In *The Study of Coalition Behavior*, edited by S. Groennings et al. New York: Holt, Rinehart and Winston, 1970.

Fiorina, M., and C. Plott. "Committee Decisions under Majority Rule: An Experimental Study." *American Political Science Review* 72 (June 1978): 575–98.

Hamburger, H. "N-person Prisoner's Dilemma." *Journal of Mathematical Sociology* 3 (1973): 27–48.

Horowitz, A., and A. Rapoport. "Test of the Kernel and Two Bargaining Set Models in Four- and Five-Person Games." In *Game Theory as a*

Theory of Conflict Resolution, edited by A. Rapoport, pp. 161–92. Boston: D. Reidel, 1974.

Howard, N. *Paradoxes of Rationality: Theory of Metagames and Political Behavior*. Cambridge, Mass.: M.I.T. Press, 1971.

Leiserson, M. "Game Theory and the Study of Coalition Behavior." In *The Study of Coalition Behavior*, edited by S. Groennings et al. New York: Holt, Rinehart and Winston, 1970.

Luce, R. D., and H. Raiffa. *Games and Decisions*. New York: Wiley, 1957.

McCaleb, T. "The Size Principle and Collective Consumption Payoffs to Political Coalitions." *Public Choice* 17 (Spring 1974): 107–09.

McDonald, J. *Strategy in Poker, Business and War*. New York: Norton, 1950.

McKelvey, R., P. Ordeshook, and M. Winer. "The Competitive Solution for N-Person Games Without Transferable Utility, With an Application to Committee Games." *American Political Science Review* 72 (June 1978): 599–615.

Oliver, P. "Selective Incentives in an Apex Game." *Journal of Conflict Resolution* 24 (March 1980): 113–41.

Olson, M., and R. Zeckhauser. "An Economic Theory of Alliances." In *Economic Theories of International Politics*, edited by B. Russett, pp. 25–45. Chicago: Markham, 1968.

Ordeshook, R. ed. *Game Theory and Political Science*. New York: New York University Press, 1978.

Rapoport, A. *Fights, Games, and Debates*. Ann Arbor, Mich.: University of Michigan Press, 1960.

———. *Two-Person Game Theory: The Essential Ideas*. Ann Arbor, Mich.: University of Michigan Press, 1966.

———. *N-Person Game Theory: Concepts and Applications*. Ann Arbor, Mich.: University of Michigan Press, 1970.

Riker, W. "A New Proof of the Size Principle." In *Mathematical Applications in Political Science*, vol. 2, edited by J. Bernd, pp. 167–74. Dallas: Southern Methodist University Press, 1967.

———. *The Theory of Political Coalitions*. New Haven, Conn.: Yale University Press, 1962.

——— and W. Zovoina. "Rational Behavior in Politics: Evidence from a Three-Person Game." *American Political Science Review* 64 (March 1970): 48–60.

Shepsle, K. "Institutional Arrangements and Equilibrium in Multidimensional Voting Models." *American Journal of Political Science* 23 (January 1979): 25–59.

Schrodt, P. "Richardson's N-Nation Model and the Balance of Power." *American Journal of Political Science* 22 (May 1978): 364–90.

Shubik, M. "Game Theory and the Study of Social Behavior." In *Game Theory and Related Approaches to Social Behavior*, edited by M. Shubik, pp. 3–77. New York: John Wiley, 1964.

Straffin, P., Jr. "The Bandwagon Curve." *American Journal of Political Science* 21 (November 1977): 695–709.

Taylor, M. "On the Theory of Government Coalition Formation." *British Journal of Political Science* 2 (July 1972): 361–73.

Von Neumann, J., and O. Morgenstern. *Theory of Games and Economic Behavior.* 2nd ed. Princeton, N.J.: Princeton University Press, 1947.

Weingast, B. "A Rational Choice Perspective on Congressional Norms." *American Journal of Political Science* 23 (May 1979): 245–62.

III Political Studies: Minimum Winning Coalitions

Brenner, S. "Minimum Winning Coalitions on the U.S. Supreme Court." *American Politics Quarterly* 7 (July 1979): 384–92.

Butterworth, R. "A Research Note on the Size of Winning Coalitions." *American Political Science Review* 65 (September 1971): 741–45.

Giles, M. "Equivalent versus Minimum Winning Opinion Size." *American Journal of Political Science* 21 (May 1977): 405–08. See comment by Rohde, same volume.

Hardin, R. "Hollow Victory: The Minimum Winning Coalition." *American Political Science Review* 70 (December 1976): 1002–04. See also "Communications." *American Political Science Review* 71 (September 1977): 1056–61.

Hinckley, B. "Coalitions in Congress: Size and Ideological Distance." *Midwest Journal of Political Science* 16 (May 1972): 197–207.

———. "Coalitions in Congress: Size in a Series of Games." *American Politics Quarterly* 1 (July 1973): 339–59.

Koehler, D. "The Legislative Process and the Minimum Winning Coalition." In *Probability Models of Collective Decision Making*, edited by R. Niemi and H. Weisberg. Columbus, Ohio: Charles Merrill, 1972.

———. "Legislative Coalition Formation: the Meaning of Minimum Winning Size with Uncertain Participation." *Midwest Journal of Political Science* 19 (February 1975): 27–39.

Lutz, D., and R. Murray. "Coalition Formation in the Texas Legislature: Issues, Payoffs, and Winning Coalition Size." *Western Political Quarterly* 28 (June 1975): 296–315.

Lutz, D., and J. Williams. *Minimum Coalitions in Legislatures: A Review of the Evidence.* Sage Professional Paper 04-028. Beverly Hills and London: Sage Publications, January 1976.

Meltz, D. "Legislative Party Cohesion: A Model of the Bargaining Process in State Legislatures." *Journal of Politics* 35 (August 1973): 649–81.

Murray, R., and D. Lutz. "Redistricting Decisions in the American States: A Test of the Minimum Winning Coalition Hypothesis." *American Journal of Political Science* 18 (May 1974): 233–57.

Rohde, D. "Policy Goals and Opinion Coalitions in the Supreme Court." *Midwest Journal of Political Science* 16 (May 1972): 208–24.

———. "A Theory of the Formation of Opinion Coalitions in the U.S. Supreme Court." In *Probability Models of Collective Decision-Making*, edited by R. Niemi and H. Weisberg. Columbus, Ohio: Charles Merrill, 1972.

Shepsle, K. "On the Size of Winning Coalitions." *American Political Science Review* 68 (June 1974): 505–18. See Butterworth comment and Shepsle reply, same volume.

Southwold, M. "Riker's Theory and the Analysis of Coalitions in Precolonial Africa." In *The Study of Coalition Behavior*, edited by S. Groennings et al. New York: Holt, Rinehart and Winston, 1970.

IV Other Political Studies of Coalitions*

Adrian C., and C. Press. "Decision Costs in Coalition Formation." *American Political Science Review* 62 (June 1968): 556–63.

Almond, G., et al. *Crisis, Choice and Change*. Boston: Little, Brown, 1973.

Browne, E. "Testing Theories of Coalition Formation in the European Context." *Comparative Political Studies* 3 (January 1971): 391–412.

———. *Coalition Theories: A Logical and Empirical Critique*. Sage Professional Papers in Comparative Politics 4: 01–043. Beverly Hills and London: Sage Publications, 1973.

——— and K. Feste. "Qualitative Dimensions of Coalition Payoffs." *American Behavioral Scientist* 18 (March/April 1975): 530–56.

Browne, E., and M. Franklin. "Aspects of Coalition Payoffs in European Parliamentary Democracies." *American Political Science Review* 67 (June 1973): 453–69.

Budge, I., and V. Herman. "Coalitions and Government Formation: An Empirically Relevant Theory." *British Journal of Political Science* 8 (October 1978): 459–77.

Bueno de Mesquita, B. *Strategy, Risk and Personality in Coalition Politics: The Case of India*. Cambridge: Cambridge University Press, 1975.

Clark, T. "Catholics, Coalitions, and Policy Outputs." In *Urban Problems and Public Policy*, edited by R. Lineberry and L. Masotti, pp. 65–78. Lexington, Mass.: D. C. Heath, 1975.

———. "The Irish Ethic and the Spirit of Patronage." *Ethnicity* 2 (1975): 305–59.

Damgaard, E. "Party Coalitions in Danish Law-Making, 1953–1970." *European Journal of Political Research* 1 (April 1973): 35–66.

DeSwaan, A. *Coalition Theories and Cabinet Formation*. San Francisco: Jossey-Bass, 1974.

---

*Many of these studies include a treatment of minimum winning coalitions as one major component of several.

Dodd, L. *Coalitions in Parliamentary Government*. Princeton, N.J.: Princeton University Press, 1976.

———. "Party Coalitions in Multiparty Parliaments: A Game Theoretic Analysis." *American Political Science Review* 68 (September 1974): 1093–117.

Felsenthal, D. "Aspects of Coalition Payoffs: The Case of Israel." *Comparative Political Studies* 12 (July 1979): 151–68.

Gerston, L., J. Burnstein, and S. Cohen. "Presidential Nominations and Coalition Theory." *American Politics Quarterly* 7 (April 1979): 175–97.

Hill, P. *A Theory of Political Coalitions in Simple and Policy Making Situations*. Sage Professional Papers in American Politics. I: 04–008. Beverly Hills and London: Sage Publications, 1973.

Hinckley, B. "The Initially Strongest Player: Coalition Games and Presidential Nominations." *American Behavioral Scientist* 18 (March/April 1975): 497–512.

———. " 'Stylized' Opposition in the House of Representatives: The Effects of Coalition Behavior." *Legislative Studies Quarterly* 2 (February 1977): 5–28.

———. "Twenty-One Variables Beyond the Size of Winning Coalitions." *Journal of Politics* 41 (February 1979): 192–212.

Kessel, J. *The Goldwater Coalition*. Indianapolis: Bobbs-Merrill, 1968.

Leiserson, M. "Factions and Coalitions in One-Party Japan." *American Political Science Review* 62 (September 1968): 770–87.

Li, R., and B. Hinckley. "Time Series, Systems Analysis, and Serial Dependence in Coalition Formation." *Political Methodology* (Winter 1976): 523–44.

Manley, J. "The Conservative Coalition in Congress." *American Behavioral Scientist* 17 (November/December 1973): 223–47.

McGregor, E., Jr. "Uncertainty and National Nominating Coalitions." *Journal of Politics* 40 (November 1978): 1011–42.

Norpoth, H. "Choosing a Coalition Partner: Mass Preferences and Elite Decision in West Germany." *Comparative Political Studies* 12 (January 1980): 424–40.

Russett, B. "Components of an Operational Theory of International Alliance Formation." *Journal of Conflict Resolution* 12 (September 1968): 285–301.

Sapiro, V. "Sex and Games: On Oppression and Rationality." *British Journal of Political Science* 9 (October 1979): 385–408.

Schneider, J. *Ideological Coalitions in Congress*. Westport, Conn.: Greenwood Press, 1979.

Starr, H. *War Coalitions: The Distributions of Payoffs and Losses*. Lexington, Mass.: D. C. Heath, 1972.

Ting, W. P. Y. "Coalitional Behavior Among the Chinese Military Elite." *American Political Science Review* 73 (June 1979): 478–93.

Uslaner, E. "A Contextual Model of Coalition Formation in Congress." *American Behavioral Scientist* 18 (March/April 1975): 513–29.

————. "Partisanship and Coalition Formation in Congress." *Political Methodology* 2 (Fall 1975): 381–414.

Warwick, P. "The Durability of Coalition Governments in Parliamentary Democracy." *Comparative Political Studies* 11 (January 1979): 465–98.

Wood, D., and J. Pitzer. "Parties, Coalitions, and Cleavages: A Comparison of Two Legislatures in Two French Republics." *Legislative Studies Quarterly* 4 (May 1979): 197–226.

Zais, J., and J. Kessel. "A Theory of Presidential Nominations with a 1968 Illustration." In *Perspectives on Presidential Selection*, edited by D. Matthews, pp. 120–42. Washington, D.C.: The Brookings Institution, 1973.

V Collections of Studies

Cotter, C., ed. *Political Science Annual*, vol. 4. Indianapolis: Bobbs-Merrill, 1973.

Groennings, S., et al., eds. *The Study of Coalition Behavior*. New York: Holt, Rinehart and Winston, 1970.

Hinckley, B., ed. "Coalitions and Time: Crossdisciplinary Studies." *American Behavioral Scientist* 18 (March/April 1975). Reprinted as *Coalitions and Time*. Beverly Hills and London: Sage Publications, 1976.

Niemi, R., and H. Weisberg, eds. *Probability Models of Collective Decision Making*. Columbus, Ohio: Charles Merrill, 1972. See especially pp. 1–20, 101–78.

Ordeshook, P., ed. *Game Theory and Political Science*. New York: New York University Press, 1978.

Rapoport, A., ed. *Game Theory as a Theory of Conflict Resolution*. Boston: D. Reidel, 1974.

Index

international coalitions and, 130–31, 134*n*, 138–43
n-person games, 27–29
payoff matrix in, 23
political convention and, 30–31
problems in political application of, 40–42, 46
rationality in, 23
time dimension and, 65–66
two-person games, 24–26
Gamson, William, 4, 16, 19, 20, 34, 35, 44, 68, 103, 106, 107
Garriga-Pico, Jose, 30
Goals, 23, 92
assumptions about, 44–46, 114
as independent variable, 59
multiple, 45–46
"Government," as not synonymous with "politics," 7, 8

H

Hierarchies (vertical linkages), 83–86, 88, 91–93
House of Representatives, United States, 73–74
Democratic Party coalition activity in, 56, 113–27

I

Ideology, 59, 63–64, 67, 140–41
Imputation, 28
Inactivity, 55, 56*n*
Incentives, 60
Incompatible coalitions, 75
Information available
as independent variable, 61–62, 64
political convention and, 97–109
See also Salient cues for decision
Instability. *See* Uncertainty
International coalitions, 74, 85, 129–43
conceptualization, 130–34
research questions and hypotheses, 134–38
variables and measures, 138–43
i-trust, Lieberman's concept of, 72–73

K

Kaplan, Abraham, 13*n*
Kessel, John, 12*n*, 33
Koehler, David, 61, 128*n*

L

Lasswell, Harold, 11*n*, 13
Learning (learned behavior), 68–73, 113
Legislative coalitions, 13
See also Political party activity, legislative
Lieberman, Bernhardt, 12*n*, 54, 72–74
Likeness among players, 59
international coalitions and, 140–41
Linkages
applying the analysis of, 92–94
in boundary situations, 88–90
horizontal, 86–88
overlapping membership and, 90–92
vertical, 83–86
Linked triads, Caplow on, 75, 82–90, 92, 94
Luce, R. Duncan, 22–23, 29

M

Manley, John, 13*n*, 33
Matching, of control group and subjects, 39
McKelvey, 30
Measurement, 43
international coalitions and 138–43
legislative coalitions and, 114–16
Media, 104–06
Membership, overlapping. *See* Overlapping membership
Membership change, 90–91
Membership selection, 91–92
Membership turnover, congressional, 127
Minimum-power theory, 19, 20, 68
Minimum-resource theory, 19–22, 34, 35, 68, 69
Minimum winning coalitions, 18, 19, 21–22, 29–31, 34, 40, 56
time dimension and, 66–67
Minimum winning perceptions, 102, 103, 106, 108
Mixed-motive situation, 5, 7–9
definition of, 4

Morgenstern, O., 22
Morris, Roger, 89

N

Natural political settings
  alliances in, 131–34
  research in, 42–47
    assumptions about goals, 44–46
    coalition players, 44
    coalition situations, 43–44
New York Times, 104–06
Niemi, Richard, 59
Nominations. *See* Political nominations
Non-constant-sum games, 24n
Non-zero-sum games, 24
Norms, group, 60, 72
N-person games, 24–25, 27–30, 63, 93
Nuclear test ban treaty, U.S.-Soviet, 12, 54

O

Olson, Mancur, Jr., 136n
Overlapping membership, 81–82, 88, 90–92
  as independent variable, 59
  in international coalitions, 141, 143
  See also Linkages

P

Parity of resources, 55
Parties. *See* Political party activity
Partner
  bargaining, initial choice of
    extent of initial advantage and, 98–108
    information available and, 98–109
  coalition. *See* Coalition partner
Payoff matrix, 23–26, 53, 60
Payoffs
  convertible, 76–78
  distribution of, as dependent variable, 54–55
  in game theory, 23–26, 28, 31
  from international coalitions, 136, 142, 143
  of war, 136, 142, 143
"Peer coalitions" (horizontal linkages), 83, 86–88, 91–93

Players
  coalition. *See* Coalition players in games, 23
Political convention
  empirical political studies and, 34–35
  game theory and, 30–31
  information available and, 97–109
  social-psychological studies and, 21–22
  See also Political nomination
Political Decision Questionnaire, 97–99
Political environment, coalitions in, 81–94
  See also Linkages
Political nominations, 30–31, 35–36, 58
  presidential. *See* Presidential nominations
Political party activity, legislative, 111–28
  as coalition activity, 116–26
    coalition activity and inactivity, 117–18
    importance and decline, 118–20
    presidential effects, 120–27
  conceptualization, 111–14
  measurement, 114–16
Power
  application or exercise of, 4–9, 13
  balance of, 129, 134, 136–39
  definitions of, 4n
  dictatorial, 77
  distribution (power rankings)
    Caplow's notion of, 16–17, 82, 85, 139
    international, 139, 140, 143
  See also Minimum-power theory
Presidential nominations, 12, 57, 63–64, 105–07
  empirical studies of, 33–35, 44
  See also Political convention
Presidential party, congressional coalition activity and, 120–27

R

Raiffa, H., 22–23
Random choice, 20, 34, 35, 68, 69, 103, 106, 107
Randomization, 39
Ranney, Austin, 6n
Recurrence of the game, 62
Repetitive games, 69, 71–72, 78–79
  combined cumulative games and, 76–77
  international alliances and, 137

Variables (*cont.*)
   dependent, 53–57, 92, 134, 136, 143
   independent, 53, 57–62, 81, 134–36
   international coalitions and, 134–43
   time dimension and, 70–71
Variable sum games, 24n
Verisimilitude, 38–40, 43
Vinacke, W. E., 18
Von Neumann, J., 22

W

Wallace, Michael, 133
War, 134–36, 138
   distribution of payoffs of, 136, 142, 143

Weingast, Barry, 128n
Weisband, Edward, 76n
Winning, attitudes toward, 59–60

Y

Yarwood, Dean, 13n

Z

Zais, James, 12n
Zeckhauser, Richard, 136n
Zero-sum games, 24, 25, 29, 34, 73n

A B C D E F G H I J
1 2 3 4 5 6 7 8 9